Belkacem Belmekki & Michel Naumann

Paradoxes of Pakistan: A Glimpse

Belkacem Belmekki & Michel Naumann

PARADOXES OF PAKISTAN: A GLIMPSE

Bibliografische Information der Deutschen Nationalbibliothek
Die Deutsche Nationalbibliothek verzeichnet diese Publikation in der Deutschen Nationalbibliografie; detaillierte bibliografische Daten sind im Internet über http://dnb.d-nb.de abrufbar.

Bibliographic information published by the Deutsche Nationalbibliothek
Die Deutsche Nationalbibliothek lists this publication in the Deutsche Nationalbibliografie; detailed bibliographic data are available in the Internet at http://dnb.d-nb.de.

ISBN-13: 978-3-8382-1603-4
© *ibidem* Press, Stuttgart 2022
Alle Rechte vorbehalten

Das Werk einschließlich aller seiner Teile ist urheberrechtlich geschützt. Jede Verwertung außerhalb der engen Grenzen des Urheberrechtsgesetzes ist ohne Zustimmung des Verlages unzulässig und strafbar. Dies gilt insbesondere für Vervielfältigungen, Übersetzungen, Mikroverfilmungen und elektronische Speicherformen sowie die Einspeicherung und Verarbeitung in elektronischen Systemen.

All rights reserved. No part of this publication may be reproduced, stored in or introduced into a retrieval system, or transmitted, in any form, or by any means (electronical, mechanical, photocopying, recording or otherwise) without the prior written permission of the publisher. Any person who does any unauthorized act in relation to this publication may be liable to criminal prosecution and civil claims for damages.

Printed in the EU

TABLE OF CONTENTS

INTRODUCTION 7
CHAPTER I: HISTORY BEFORE PAKISTAN 13
    The Quest for Unity 14
    Islam in India 18
    The Mughal Empire 25
    Colonization 32

CHAPTER II: THE FOUNDING FATHERS OF PAKISTAN 37
    Sayyid Ahmad Khan 39
    Muhammad Iqbal: the dream of Pakistan and the Islamic
        Renaissance: 45
    Muhammad Ali Jinnah: 55

CHAPTER III: THE HISTORY OF PAKISTAN 71
    The Politicians and Founding Fathers 72
    The Generals and the Bureaucrats 75
    A Decade of Alternation 80
    Pakistan in the Twenty-First Century 82

CONCLUSION 89

BIBLIOGRAPHY 95

APPENDIXES 97
    Jinnah's 14 points established in 1929 about the coming
        independence of India 97
    Jinnah and the Constitution of Pakistan: 99
    Cardinal Coutts on Minorities in Pakistan (11/8/2019) 105

INTRODUCTION

In 1947 the territory of colonial India was split in two countries, Pakistan and India. The second one had the certainty to reconnect with its pre-colonial history through a deep anti-colonial struggle admired in the whole world because of Gandhi's non-violent and moral figure. These roots, reinforced by the feeling of a Hindu nation responsible for the protection of the Great Goddess' body within its established sedentary borders, produced a formal democracy full of ambiguities of course but not deprived of qualities and self-confidence. Pakistan is a more ambiguous case: the country came from a break from the original body (colonial India). This partition intended to move towards a pure nation of Muslims. Many people had to migrate from India to reach Pakistan. The identity of this new entity is of course less rooted and settled in its borders than India in so far as the next creative move towards purity for the Pakistani people might be towards the religious ideals connected with the far away holy lands of Mecca, Medina, Jerusalem or even towards what can occur anywhere in the Islamic world. Purity has no motherland, it is not rooted, it is a spiritual reality. India is somewhere, even her spirituality is connected with the landscape; Pakistan is somewhere and somewhere else.

Pakistan has subsequently gone through complex processes of research, splits (originally Pakistan was composed of a Western and an Eastern unit but the second one, Eastern Bengal, left the union after a quarter of a century of common life in a difficult union of these two components), political struggles, problems due to the diversity of the country, constitutional changes, contradictory sources of inspiration and international connections... To some it is a miracle that such a nation (or perhaps should we say a protonation) could survive and even progress in a situation of crisis which has been and remains almost permanent. We should however remember that crisis means "choice" and that it does not imply stagnation. Pakistan is a paradox and, as such, a country at a crossroad where almost all the roads of the present world converge. A paradox but a complex, rich and dynamic one and a most interesting one!

The name Pakistan refers to its components: **P**unjab, the **A**fghan province (the North-West of the colony), **K**ashmir, **S**indh and Baluchi**stan**. It is the successful creation of a group of Cambridge students led by Chaudhry Ramat Ali (1897–1951). It appeared first in 1933 in a pamphlet calling for independence and entitled *Now or Never*. Strangely enough Bengal is missing although it became Eastern Pakistan (nowadays' Bangladesh). In 1947 the country counted 75 million inhabitants (42 million in the Eastern part) for a surface of 935,000 square kilometres (only 100,000 km² for the Eastern part). The primary sector (agriculture) was promising as Punjab (21 million) with the Indus and its confluents was a rich agricultural region that produced almost 50 % of the wheat of the English colony of India. Sindh (4,600,00 inhabitants) produced rice and cotton. The Western half of the country had a rich pastoral economy in the Afghan province (5 million inhabitants) and Baluchistan (slightly less than one million). Coal in the north of Punjab and petrol struck in Rawalpindi, in the same province, and the wealth of Baluchistan (coal and gas in addition to zinc, iron and copper) did not make the country self-reliant as far as energy was concerned and industries were scarce in 1947: some 20 cotton textile factories (against 900 in India), ten sugar plants (against 156 in India), no weaving factories of jute. Hyderabad (Sindh) was the starting point of a railway going northwards and eastwards and from Karachi a line reached Quetta, the Balochi capital in the far west. The Afghan province had a road between Peshawar and Kabul (the capital of Afghanistan) and the Khyber Pass was the link between the two countries. Karachi, the capital of Pakistan in 1947 (110,000 inhabitants), near the Indus Delta, was a port and an airport connected to the Middle-East and the Far-East.

Pakistan has courted diversity both as a gift and a risk as we can see when describing the country in the twenty-first century:

- 796 096 square kilometres; 210 million of inhabitants (51 % are rural folks); the demographic growth is around 3.1 % per year. Like most third World countries the population is growing and the young form a most important part of it.

- The natural and regional geography is not easy as floods and earthquakes are frequent: floods in 1950 (3000 dead), hurricane in 1970 (half a million victims), earthquake in 1974 (100 000 people left without a home, 5000 dead), a drought in 2000, earthquake in Kashmir in 2005, hurricane in 2007 on the coasts, floods in 2010 (1800 dead, 20 millions of victims), flood in the South of Pakistan (Sindh and Baluchistan) in 2011, violent rains and earthquake (Baluchistan) in 2013, heatwaves due to global warming…[1]
- Pakistan shares dangerous borders with Iran, Afghanistan, India, China and has a coast on the Arabian Sea (such an environment has constantly been haunted by threats of wars and Pakistan has been involved in several conflicts with India).
- Its diplomacy (influenced by the nuclear power status of Pakistan, India, and China) must conciliate China and the United States.
- The Pakistani people are divided into several ethnic components (Punjabis and Saraikis, Pashtuns, Sindhis, Muhajirs, Baluchis) and languages (English, Urdu, Punjabi, Sindhi, Saraiki — the language of a northern ethnic group of Punjab-, Pashto and Baluchi).
- Many religious traditions live together in the Islamic Republic of Pakistan (Sunnis, Shi'ites, Zoroastrians, Hindus, Sikhs, Christians, Animists…).
- The regional components are very difficult to handle for the centre: the mountainous west of western Pakistan is opposed to the rich Indus plain that produces rice and other cereals thanks to irrigation and the generous monsoons (June–September); the eastern half of western Pakistan is divided between the north (Punjab) and the south (Sindh).
- The historical destiny of such a country is connected to world powers like the US and China, Central Asia, the Delhi plain, the Himalayas, the Third World, the Islamic world and the Middle East.

---

[1] Tasmin Altaf Butt, *Pakistan*, De Boeck, Louvain-la-Neuve, 2014, p 42.

- Tensions between the bourgeois, the bureaucratic and the feudal sectors of the élite have not been solved yet.
- The country's budget tends to ignore the poorer sections of the people and the peripheric regions of the country.
- Left wing planned efforts to correct injustice go against the liberal main stream of the twenty-first century that favours the trickling down effect according to which success for a few finally reaches the unsuccessful.
- An almost 6 % growth is nevertheless a remarkable achievement but the economy remains fragile because of contradictions such as the existence of a legal and a mafia economy. It is also endangered by corruption, debts and ecological problems...
- The diaspora of overseas Pakistanis is estimated around 7–8 million: workers in the Gulf, qualified people in the States, an already old community in Britain known from the very famous Brick Lane, sometimes presented as a part of Pakistan transplanted in England... They probably send 10 to 15 billion $ to the motherland every year.
- Migrants are many in Pakistan: Afghan refugees come first and Bangladeshis second (mainly in Karachi where they tend to mix with the Muhajirs of the partition); central Asians are very diverse (Uzbeks, Tajiks, Iranians); Arabs and Birmans are also quite important.
- Displaced Pakistanis (mostly from Khyber Pakhtunkhwa) are probably under one million. The informal economic sector is strengthened by these insecure people transplanted far from home.

Pakistan is a microcosm of the whole world and almost the sum of the problems of the whole world. This is why trying to approach and study such a complex country is a challenge but the reward might be enlightening for our time.

We will define three different periods in our search:

- Before Pakistan: complex historical factors coming from the past have been loaded on Pakistan's cradle when the new

entity came to life. They will be the object of the first chapter.
- The Muslim Indian world and the growth and birth of Pakistan were the key dynamic forces that carved the country during the lull between the past and the future. (1857–1947)
- Ordeals and efforts of the new nation in its difficult environment will be studied in the last chapter as a consequence of the past and of the features of the entity created under the name of Pakistan.

We hope to be able then to assess slightly more accurately the reality that is called Pakistan and its significance for our world.

CHAPTER I: HISTORY BEFORE PAKISTAN

The original communism of the groups of human beings who populated the earth slowly started changing when the warming up of the climate of the twelfth millennium created better conditions of growth. Before this turning point in human history, Palaeolithic groups had lived in what is now Pakistan from 3 million of years before Christ. Punjab was already an important region for human activities and prehistoric industries. Baluchistan was the cradle of the Mehrgarh culture between 7000 BC and 2600 BC. Climate changes might have been responsible for a shift which made the Indus Valley more attractive. Then new tools, the invention of agriculture and cattle breeding, increased exchanges, more populous communities favoured hierarchies and structures of work division and decision making that were to create inequalities ultimately sustained by state formations.

In southern Asia city-states emerged in the space now called Pakistan, in and around the Indus Valley which provided a rich agricultural basis for urbanization (fourth–second millennium). These towns were built of bricks and well planned with an elaborate system of gutters and huge tanks for the monsoon water. Seals found by the archaeologists prove that they had commercial relations with Mesopotamia and Persia, two cultural zones which are still connected with Pakistan. The Dravidians of South India have linguistic and iconic arguments to claim that this Indus civilization was one of their achievements but the debate is still going on. If the traditional theories about the Aryan invasion used to pretend that Indo-European tribes from the North-West (Ukraine) destroyed this culture around 1500 BC, modern historians rather think that a discrepancy between the agricultural base and the demands of cities as well as a shrinking of the trade incomes were responsible for what has actually been a slow and peaceful decay.

The new historians also think that the Aryans may be the speakers of related languages, but they hardly have any proof that they were a race. The present tendency is to consider that India and Pakistan were inhabited by very diverse peoples and cultures. If

China was politically united by two powerful rivers that flow from west to east, such a configuration does not exist in India. The gathering of tribes, sedentary and nomadic groups, various races and religions rather comes from the use by some priests of scattered cultural elements to create a loose ideological unity which was to become what we know nowadays as Hinduism. The prestige of this clergy (the ancestors of nowadays' Brahmins), probably more important in deltas and rich plains than in forests and mountains, was so contagious that many classes imitated their habits of endogamy (marriage in the caste) and became first rigid classes and later exclusive castes. The caste system was based on the ideology of *karma*: a pariah or the member of a very low caste could only explain this unfortunate position by interpreting it as the consequence of the sins of past lives. Nevertheless, resistance and revolts occurred, which we can only guess because written official documents would hide such subversive movements. The élites have always known that memories of the past determine present history.

The Quest for Unity

During the Bronze Age the west of northern India prevailed because of its copper mines but the Iron age (from the tenth century in India) was definitely eastern and strong states appeared in what is nowadays Bihar and Bengal.[2] The iron tools were so efficient that individuals depended less from the collective work of villagers and the iron weapons strengthened armies and kings. In a more competitive, unequal and ferocious world the hegemony of Brahmanism was shattered: hedonism and materialism became important philosophical trends and Jainism developed acetic attitudes of rejection of worldly ambitions that showed that traditional social achievements were no longer blindly accepted. Between these two trends the middle way proposed by Buddhism seduced warriors tired of priestly hegemony, merchants whose long travels were seen as a cause of impurity due to contacts with strangers, silenced

---

[2] Bhairabi Prasad Sahu, *Iron and Social Change in Early India,* OUP, New Delhi, 2006.

women, poor folks who were often remedied and helped by charitable Buddhist monks and whoever was a victim of the greed and violence of the competing states. The period was also a time of growth of the international trade. Egypt, Phoenician and Greek cities, Ethiopia and, later, Rome reached the Indian coasts by sea and the Persian Empire had reached India through the mountains of Pakistan. Buddhism saw with more tolerance than the Brahmin priests the relations with foreign powers and the trade with faraway lands.

When these relations happened to become dangerous, the connection between the Buddhists and the warriors was most important because they were obviously the group who could go beyond the ideological unity proposed by the Brahmins and unite politically the subcontinent. This task became very urgent when the Greeks of Alexander the Great crossed the mountains of Western Pakistan, populated by tribes like present day Pashtuns, to reach the states of the Indus plains. A Khalash legend presents this ethnic group of a few thousand persons as the descents of Alexander's army. Actually, they might have Euro-Mediterranean features. They were farmers and cattle-breeders and their isolation in the mountains allowed them to keep their polytheistic creed and their seasonal rituals.[3] Although the Macedonian conqueror, Alexander, after defeating the Indian prince Poros, withdrew, a bit later, Euthydemus and Monandrous created Greek states in the Bactrian and Sogdian regions and in the East of Iran. Chandragupta Maurya, backed by the Indian Machiavelli, Chanaya, who, although a Brahmin, displayed flexibility and a vision shared by the Buddhists, defeated the Greeks and a Buddhist, Ashoka, became emperor of unified India in 268 BC.

Pakistan also witnessed during these years the flowering of a Greek and Buddhist culture that makes us think that the vocation of this region of the subcontinent might be more a syncretic one than a rigidly defined one. The Sakes (a group of Scythes) in the time of Christ and the nomads from the East whose dynasties later

---

[3] Nowadays they are, like their Shi'ite neighbours, threatened by the Taliban who want to convert them to Sunnite Islam.

prevailed in the region, the Kushanas (first AD century), remained faithful to this openness, especially under the reign of king Kanisha. On the other hand, the Mauryan achievement was not long lasting. India was still too diverse. Regions and cultures out of the main stream resisted the trend set by Asoka whose spies and bureaucrats became increasingly unpopular and a coup d'état in 178 BC removed the Maurya king in favours of a Brahmin Dynasty.

The unity of India became purely nominal. In the third century the Buddhist Kuchana of the east lost the hegemony on northern India to the Hindu Gupta of the west. This new Dynasty was shattered by the Huns in the late fifth century but king Harsha (606–647) restored the power of the Guptas. The descendants of the Huns became the Rajput princes of the West who were knights and champions of Hinduism. After Harsha, India was not reunited and the Guptas centred their power on Bengal. Their last attempt to restore their hegemony was ruined by the wars led by the Kashmiri king Lalitadya (733–769). Even Bengal was lost by the Guptas when a commoner, Gopala, founded there the pro-Buddhist Palas Dynasty, only displaced by the Sena Dynasty in 1125.

These geographical and political divisions gave birth to a feudal society. As India was more and more divided her mainstream religion became the source of a spiritual unity that prevailed on political unity. Hinduism led an ideological crusade against Buddhism that shrunk tremendously. The language of the so-called Aryans, Sanskrit, became a prestigious but elitist medium. With Sankara the philosophical forms of Brahmanism were strengthened: *"only the Brahman is real; the universe is not real and the individual soul is nothing but the universal Soul."*[4] With Feudalism and against the high-flown intellectuality of philosophers like Sankara, the cattle-breeders (with Krishna as the main God) and the farmers (with Shiva as the main God) developed religious trends of emotional devotion (*Bahkti*) to a chosen God to whom the believer was like a vassal. The Bahkti is deeply rooted in the local experiences of the

---

4   Quotation from Marcel Sauton's introduction to his translation of Sankara: *Le plus beau fleuron de la discrimination*, Maisonneuve, Paris, 1946.

people whereas Sankara's philosophical works served the Brahmin élite.

The impression left by our survey of this historical period is that the unification of the subcontinent could only come from Buddhism but in the process state constraints were checked by the diversity of India, thus creating a renewal of Hinduism and a growth of feudal forces. Whereas the imperial state could not give a positive answer to the contradiction between unity and diversity, the local level and also the cultural level have been more successful in dealing with it. In a world of villages and self-sufficient regions any religion took local forms. In Bengal the villages have always been enlightened by local saints and mystics often springing from the poorest sections of the population. Each caste had its own culture and memory. The outcastes created forms and cultures of resistance as dacoits (bandits) or non-violent resisting communities. The invaders (Greeks, Sakes, Huns…) who came through the passes of the mountainous western half of nowadays' Pakistan had always been integrated to the cultures of the subcontinent. The meeting of Greek and Buddhist cultures into a unique Greek and Buddhist culture and the local tolerance of differences can be seen as proof of a real genius to preserve peace and openness in a dynamic whole deprived of state constraints. The continuity of this trend through centuries shows that this is a cultural and a historical feature which is not to be ignored.

What also strikes us is that the territory nowadays called Pakistan did not produce a centre that determined its destiny. Connected to Hinduism and India, Persia, central Asia, the Greeks, the Sakes, the Huns, Buddhism, China, the seas of the Indian ocean, it is everything but a centralized growing energy. Sindh, for instance, was part, with the Rai Dynasty of the Greek and Buddhist zone of influence, but the Persian Empire was often most influential, if not the suzerain of Sindh, so that a strong Zoroastrian presence could be felt. The region nowadays called Pakistan was a multi-centred world created by many different sources of energy. Should Pakistan choose a myth to define her destiny, it would not be the Indus civilization that serves the Dravidians better to enhance their identity, it would not be Asoka or the Gupta kingdom that serve India better, not the Greek and Buddhist reality created by the Rai Dynasty in Sindh, it can only be the original local diversity and syncretism that ten centuries of history show as the most obvious logic of regional construction. The philosophy of such diversity cannot be a finalistic vision that implies that, through a unifying and progressive process the various units of the whole would lose part of their originality and drop most of the paths that they had explored so that they could join the main stream to reach a definite End and a single identity. We must prefer to the process towards a final historical point a Spinozian vision of growth in all the directions instead of a single one. This type of growth is more open but not without its own conception of unity. It is a very subtle, complex and high-flown totality which, like God, cannot be defined because it is too rich and too open to be imprisoned in concepts coming from the tongue of Babel and the authority of strong kings like Nimrud. It is a richest way of understanding the space that we now call Pakistan than a teleological finality.

Then Islam appeared as another unifying trend. As a religion born out of a process of gathering tribes and cities into a nation in Arabia, it could fulfil a similar mission in India but once more History showed that the contradiction between unity and diversity is much more complex than any process intended to create a state or/and a nation. Islam did go further and deeper towards unification than either the Buddhists or the Hindus, but each achievement, however impressive, was followed by a time of decay and divisions. As a consequence of its failure, Islam became much more than an ideology and a political project and it joined the many paths of diversity and freedom.

Islam in India

The Conservative vision of Islam as a predatory movement against Delhi forgets that the Sakes, Huns and Kuchana hordes, and also the Rajput and Gujarati princes attacked Northern India and the Delhi plain a long time before the Muslim Turks and Afghan coming from their mountainous strongholds. They just followed a trend due to the relations between the owners of the roof and the owners of the house. Religion has nothing to do with such a historical feature. The theory of the Muslim conquest also ignores the fact that once settled in India the Muslim rulers, like the other human groups that came from or through the mountains, became truly Indian and fulfilled a role defined by local historical realities independent of religions.

The advent and spread of Islam in Arabia soon gathered pace as the result of a move for unity whose motives were partly spiritual and partly economic and political. The mastery of the trade routes of luxury goods from the Southern coast of the peninsula to the North was an important factor. An Ethiopian and Christian conquest of Yemen had also convinced the Arabs that their clannish rivalries could not last much longer. The Roman Empire of Constantinople was also threatening the borders of Arabia. The unification was the work of Islam as a religious simplification of Christian dogmas and an attempt to settle quarrels between Jews and Christians as well as between tribes. This new creed nevertheless was a continuation of these two monotheistic religions in so far that it was a monotheistic revelation coming from the same Deity addressed to an Arab prophet, Muhammad (571–632), from the great Koreishi clan of Mecca, for the Arab people and the world humanity. Later, as the genius of this pure and clear vision could unify Western Asia, the Muslims conquered the Middle East and Egypt.

This expansion first gave the hegemony to the Arabs involved in the Middle-Eastern trade, the Omayyad Dynasty of Damas (661–750), but, the Shi'ites, linked to Ali, the Prophet's son-in-law, whose family had remained close to the equalitarian moods of the soldiers of the faith and, open to protesters, peripheric clans and cultures and also to mystic trends, prevailed in the Persian world. The new Abbasid Dynasty (650–1258), although Sunnite, stressed from Bagdad the importance of the Persian components of Islam. Divisions and splits appeared in the Empire, new states were established, often based on the revolutionary Shi'ite trend, till the Turkish soldiers of the Empire defended the threatened positions of the orthodox Sunnite Muslims against their rivals.

Some years after the passing away of Prophet Muhammad, Arabs settled peacefully in Makran (Baluchistan). In 711 Arab knights had already reached Sindh through the passes of what is now North-Western Pakistan and created two princely states: Mansura and Multan. They were far from the heart of Islam and their importance remained very limited in South Asia. Persecutions against the state religion of Iran provoked a migration of Zoroastrians who settled in present day Pakistan and India. They probably followed the routes that Jews and Christians had already used to flee from pre-Islamic Persian persecutions against them. The power of the Umayyads and later the Abbasids remained very light on the Muslim rulers of this part of the world. In 977 Shi'ites conquered Sindh and ruled it till 1352. Originally, they were Qarmats from Bahrain but soon they became the vassals of the Fatimids of Egypt who challenged the Damas Turkish Sunnites of the Middle-East. The Shi'ites were divided on the number of Imams (6, 9 or twelve and even eight) who inspired the faith till the persecuted line of these leaders connected to Ali and Muhammad's daughter Fatima became hidden to reappear one day with an Imam who would save the Community. The Agha Khan's connection with Pakistan comes from the impact of these events and the settlement of Shi'ites. The Sunnites, looking for a deeper link with the people, created a local rule by Pirs (holy men) whose authority was light and whose commitment to the interests of their particular region was extremely deep. Probably about AD 1000 the Baluchi people arrived from the Caspian Sea in South-Western Pakistan where they probably mixed with a Dravidian population. They also met Arab and Persian local populations, adopted their vision of Islam and in the eighteenth century formed the Kingdom of Kalat while retaining their clans and tribal codes.

In the eighth century the Chinese had penetrated the Hindu Kush (the Himalaya Mountains of Afghanistan and north Pakistan) and influences from the Far East were probably as strong as the influences from the Middle-East. Meanwhile the Arabs and the Persians progressed far beyond the eastern coasts of the Caspian Sea and the Chinese and Buddhist positions along the silk roads were threatened. In 751 the armies of the faithful defeated the armies of China at the battle of Talas (east of the Caspian Sea). The cause of the war was a fight between two Turkish states. One called the Calif against the other and its Chinese allies. The Tibetans and many Turks fought with the Arabs. The Chinese troops were exhausted by their long journey from home to Central Asia and during the battle their Turkish mercenaries betrayed them. The Emperor was ready to send another army but the revolt of General An Lushan obliged him not to do so and concentrate on Chinese problems. These events favoured Turkish unrest and Uighurs' attacks against the Tang Dynasty. In 950 the conversion of the Uighur, prepared by the battle of Talas and Muslim commercial activities, was a major Islamic success in Central Asia.

The stability of Central Asia was gone and the Turks became a most important political and military factor in the region that can be described as the roof of India. The situation was always changing because at any time a tribal leader could spring up, create a new conquering *asabiya*[5] and carve for himself and his devoted warriors a domain if not a kingdom or an empire. In the early eleventh century, Jayapala, the King of Und and the Undabandapuras, was defending the Indus against Sabuttigin, a Turkish slave and soldier who had become Sultan of Ghazni in Afghanistan and whose son, Mahmud conquered Punjab in 1022. Between 1001 and 1026, he invaded Northern India seventeen times. By the third decade of the eleventh century, he had an army of Turks, Afghans and Punjabis whose swift moves surprised many Indian generals. It is obvious that his purpose was not to settle in India but only to plunder this rich neighbour. Spices, jewels and luxury goods had given India the repute of a very wealthy country that attracted the bold and nomadic warlords of Afghanistan.

Mahmud's children and grandchildren, perhaps corrupted by the wealth accumulated in Ghazni, lost their father's energy[6] and in 1060 they flew out of their capital city when attacked by a slave and a soldier who had become Sultan of Ghor. This place soon produced another Turkish invader of northern India and in 1185 Muhammed of Ghor conquered Lahore and the whole of Punjab. Six

---

[5] The term comes from Ibn Khaldun and it refers to the strong identity of tribal groups and fighters.
[6] We follow here Ibn Khadun's theory on the weakening of the *asibiya* in an urban environment.

years later he reached the Ganga but was checked by a federation of Hindu princes. One year after his defeat at Taraori, he won a pitched battle (1192) at the same place and opened the door of northern India. His slave, Kutbud-Din Aibak, pushed this door and took Delhi in 1193, Gwalior in 1198, Gujarat in 1202 and even Bengal. When the Sultan of Ghor was murdered, his viceroy in India, Kutbud-Din Aibak, thought that the situation was ripe for him to become the independent ruler of Delhi (1206). The Muslims had already conquered jewels like Lahore, but these could not be their final destination. The position of a political centre was not ascribed to any of the regions that are nowadays in Pakistan. They were the first parts of the subcontinent to be in contact with the new faith, but the key position for the development of a Muslim Empire were Delhi, a very central position in the heart of a huge plain, and the very rich eastern state of Bengal.

After the period of raids and the time of conquest, came the time of settlement as a state, which was a difficult process because of the lack of rules and procedures for succession among the conquerors. Aibak did not reign very long (1206–1210). His successor was incompetent but soon replaced by a man, Iltumish (1211–1236), who had always been close to Aibak, the founder of the Delhi Sultanate. He had to subdue again the provinces of his kingdom because the system of the central government was based on tributes demanded to the local governors who had full local authority and subsequently were eager to become independent rulers. Iltumish's forty slave soldiers ruled after him and for some time supported the dead king's daughter, Bayiza, who ruled clad as a soldier and unveiled, until they disapproved of her love for an African (1640). In 1266 the Vizier Balban got rid of the hegemony of the forty masters of the state and took over to rule with an iron hand. His son was killed by raiding Mongols (1287) and his useless grandson, Kaikobad, murdered in 1290. He was replaced by an old man from the Kalji people, Firoz (1290–1296) who favoured his nephew and son in law Ala-u-Din (1296–1316). This ruler conquered Gujarat, raided the Decan, defeated the Mongols but left a chaotic kingdom. The patrimonial state created by the conquerors had failed.

Finally, the army took over and Gazi-Malik was the first ruler of the Togluk Dynasty. An honest and strict administrator, he tried to overcome the authoritarian trend of the past Delhi kings. Back from a campaign in Decan, his son killed him and reigned as Muhammed ibn Togluk (1325–1351), a severe and gifted administrator, but a cruel man. He tried to establish a new capital in the heart of India, Daulatabad, but the civil servants and the staff from the old capital were thrown unprepared on the roads to reach the new capital and the project turned into a disaster. He kept rising taxes so that many regions split and he died in the Sindh fighting one of the many revolts that plagued the kingdom. Firoz III (1351–1388), his cousin, tried wisely to rule the withered state and help farmers and villagers. When he died the governor of Malwa rejected the central power of Delhi (1392) whereas a eunuch, Malik Sarvar, carved for himself the kingdom of Jaunpor (1394). Delhi was without a ruler till the governor of Gujarat declared himself King in 1396. Two years later the Turku-Mongol master of Central Asia, Tamerlane, plundered Delhi. The efforts of the Tughluk Dynasty to create an organized and stable state had failed.

Tamerlane, a Shi'ite, established the Sayyid Dynasty in Delhi, but the Sunnites recovered the throne when the last Sayed abdicated in favours of the Lodi Dynasty. This change combined a passage from Shi'ite hegemony to Sunnite hegemony with a passage from Turkish rulers to Afghan rulers. The Lodies were Pashtuns, a most important tribe who dominated the north-western mountains and had seized Lahore in Punjab. This group represents presently 42 to 45 % of the Afghans and they are the strongest minority of Pakistan. They speak Pashto and, of course, all the languages of the places where they settled or established a Dynasty. The Pashtun code is based on honour, hospitality, courage, revenge tempered by consultation between the many sub-tribes and a sense of equality combined with a very competitive spirit. They are extremely flexible people when they have to adjust to a new environment and this quality was required to handle Delhi. The new rulers of North India reconquered the territories lost during the years of chaos at the end of the Tughluk Dynasty and Delhi was rising again as well as Lahore and the ports of the Indus and Bengal.

Islam was now at home in India. Discrimination in the fields of taxations and regulations had not disappeared but the Muslim rulers had often come to tolerate the Hindu majority, work with them, use Hindu ministers and councillors. They considered these infidels not as enemies but as countrymen. Low castes people who had converted to a creed that knows no castes had become Indian Muslims who were not descendants of Afghans, Turks or Mongols. The Sufi mystics had found their way in the hearts of many Indians seduced by the poetry of these mad lovers of God. In the fifteenth century a low caste weaver called Kabir used the emotions of the *Bakhti* and Sufism to write poems that criticized the blindness and corruption of official clergies and dogmas. He was to inspire Guru Nanak and the *Adi-Granth*, the book of the Sikhs who tried to take the best from Islam and Hinduism. These mystic trends became an important factor in the rise of Indian local languages as cultural languages. The Muslims of what is nowadays India or Pakistan were as diverse and even as divided as those of Persia and the Middle East. Some people could see this diversity as a weakness, but local people saw it as the privilege to love God the way they wanted. A famous Sufi story describes a hairdresser imagining the hairstyles he would propose to God and Moses scolds him for that incongruity but God rebukes His prophet because the love of the hairdresser was just rooted in his own experience of life.

On the coasts of the subcontinent was taking place what can be called the first globalization. It was born from the meeting of Islam and the first world power, China. The features of the cosmopolitan culture of this globalization centred on the Indian Ocean were extremely open and tolerant: the Indian Ocean trade linked East and West and it saw the rise of Arabic as the medium of this meeting of Arab, Persian, Chinese, Indian, Egyptian, Swahili (East Africans) merchants. The fleets of Zeng He sailed between Indonesia and Africa. Almost everywhere appeared a cult of saints and genies shared by Muslims, Hindus, Christian and Jews… Low caste people could start a carrier with the most unwanted and hard jobs on the docks of the ports and become self-made men. This trade brought African slaves and mercenaries to India. Some of them, like Iktiyar in Ahmadabad or Ambar in the Decan ruled important states. The success stories of other former slaves like Sayed Sultani or Sidi Bashir are also well documented. The Swahili of East Africa had great talents as sailors and their competence was required everywhere. The Sidis were a caste of Black men who colonized the Island of Janjira, made it an important port and protected it with a huge fort. Other Sidis settled in the forests of present-day Pakistan.[7] Islam was never a monolithic block that stifled people in a conventional way of life.

In the sixteenth century the Delhi Sultanate was replaced by the Mughal Empire.

The Mughal Empire

Once more Afghanistan was the cradle of a most important Dynasty. Babur was linked to the clan of Tamerlane through his father and the clan of Genghis Khan through his mother. He was also a refined cultured Persian and a poet. Leaving Ferghana, he conquered Kabul. He had views on Punjab but he went much further when a governor of Ibrahim Lodi (1517–1526) begged him to back his claims against his Lord. Babur won the battle of Panipat and conquered Delhi. The Mughal archery, cavalry and artillery gave him the victory. Instead of plundering the city, he became the first Mughal Emperor (1526–1530). His son, Humayun, lost his throne in 1544 to an Afghan (Pashtun) ruler of Bihar, Sher Khan, but after 11 years of exile, he reconquered his kingdom.

The next Mughal Emperor, Akbar (1556–1607), enlarged his possessions, established a new taxation system favourable to poor farmers, reduced the power of the *ulama* and Brahmins, defeated an Afghan protest against his unconventional vision of Islam, ruled India as an Indian and even tried to propose a new syncretic religion, the Din Ilahi. He was reputed as a very tolerant ruler who fought any kind of discrimination among his subjects. Not only the *dhimmis*, the people of the Book (a term of reference to Christians and Jews in Islamic lands) who are to be protected by the Muslim

---

[7]   UNESCO, *Histoire Générale de l'Afrique*, tome V, Présence Africaine, Paris, 1998, p 102–120.

rulers provided they pay the *jizya,* a special poll tax, but also the Hindu recognize his reign as a time of progress towards a unified nation. It seemed that the contradictions of the Delhi Sultanate had been overcome by Akbar's modern administration with 15 provinces, each with a governor and civil servants. The court language was Persian, the *ulama* recited the Sacred text in Arabic, Urdu (Hindi) was used in everyday life and as an idiom adopted by the Sufis. Bengali was the tongue of the East, the richest part of the Empire.

Akbar's reign has been invoked to prove that the Hindu / Moslem contradiction is a fake one. Unfortunately, his successors' views on religion were not as open-minded but if the thesis that there were no real problems between the children of Allah and the children of Rama is an exaggeration, the idea that Islam was the faith of the invaders and that most conflicts on the subcontinent were the results of Moslem invasions and intolerance is another exaggeration. The final battle between the Hindu State of Vijayanagar against the Moslem States of central India was not really a war of religion but a conflict caused by geo-political factors and the Moslems who fought in the Vijayanagar army prove it. There is no way to deny that there were times and places of persecution but one should not forget that peace and tolerance have no chronicles and that the Indian genius of negotiating with the other is one of the features of this part of the world.

In the seventeenth century the booming world trade of Akbar's time shrank because the gold of America was exhausted. New resources were only found in the eighteenth century. It therefore became difficult to pay the civil servants and the temptation was very strong for rulers to distribute fiefs instead of developing a modern bureaucratic administration. As a consequence, regional divisions gradually deepened because of the reinforcement of the traditional feudal forces. It is quite interesting to remark that the great Pashtun poet of the fifteenth century was Pir Richan, a mystic with a universal vision, whereas the great poet of the seventeenth, Khushal, insisted on issues connected to Pashtun identity. Thinking of the Mughal Empire as a national unit became more and more difficult. Religious divisions reappeared. After the reigns of Jahangir and Shah Jahan, the royal prince Dura Suko, tried to merge the two oceans (Islam and Hinduism) but his arrogance and strategic weaknesses made him an easy prey for his brother Aurangzeb (1658–1707), a pious Sunnite, who, although he was not as intolerant as he is believed to have been, was not comparable to Akbar. Aurangzeb was the last of the Emperors to ride all over his Empire to check corruption and punish crimes committed in his name. The Mughals were also, it seems, grasped by the huge continental block that they ruled and they made no efforts to develop a modern navy to vie with the Europeans whose commercial demands divided their territory into smaller rival states that hoped to get the best from the trade between continents that was growing and creating a new world economic system. The Empire remained alive and very impressive but decay was obviously coming. In spite of regional divisions more and more prevailing over centralization in India, the Mughals retained their nominal position of Suzerains of most states of the subcontinent.

The example of Sindh shows rather well the weakening of the Empire. In the seventeenth century the Kalhoro Dynasty ruled the region. Miya Yar Mohamed had gathered all the components of a Sindhi state. He was practically independent and his position as a vassal of the Mughal was purely nominal. The Kalhoro rulers tried to reconcile Muslims and Hindus and they were instrumental in the building of 12 dams to establish a sustainable system of irrigation.[8] Poets and mystics like Shah Abdul Latif Bithai, Sachal or Sami created a local culture whose themes (like the crave towards the Beloved) were Persian, Central Asian, Indian and universal. The Urs festivals were beyond all creeds and they started from local rejoicing (sports, music and poetry) to reach the universal. They could be considered, nowadays, as the alternative way to reach unity: to start from the grass root level to create a larger decentralized and diverse

---

[8] These dams never created the environmental (changes in the flow of rivers, climate, soils of the banks and animal population of the rivers), economic (fishermen, farmers, traders and boatmen thrown out of work as a consequence of these ecological perturbations) and political (displaced populations, quarrels between states over the water available) problems of modern dams.

country and even a cultural level which could be shared by the whole world.

At the end of the eighteenth century the Dynasty came to an end in spite of its links with the Durrani of Afghanistan. A very exacting Nawab provoked a revolt led by the Talpurs, Sindhi speaking Balochi people backed by the Mughals and the Persians. The Talpurs won the battle of Halani. (1783) The coming of this Balochi Dynasty shows that Sindh was very multicultural and cosmopolitan. Its identity always remained changing and not afraid of a diversity that, anyway, the rulers accepted. The relations to the Peacock Throne were loose as the rich Sindhi landowners and the venerated Pirs had loose relations with the ruling Dynasty of the country. A rigid long-standing centralized power and economic structure had for centuries been prevented by the changing course of the Indus River that did not give cities the time of life necessary to provide the stable foundations of a strong and lasting state. Commerce made the rulers unwilling to choose between Afghanistan, Persia and the Mughal Empire and flexibility prevailed over any rigid commitment to a strong centre. Even the castes seemed to be shaky: instead of a clear structure, there were what I would call proto-castes with the accountants of the rich landowners and the state (the Amuls), the traders (Bheirbads), the Brahmins (only third in the Sindhi caste structure), the Bhakti communities, the Guru followers and the mountain people. The Muslim majority was linked to the decentralized power of the local Pirs. The expression of the faith was mainly local and the festivals of one confession most often became the festival of all the villagers. It is only very late, with the Talpurs, that Sindh became fully independent from the Mughals. This Dynasty was to last a bit longer than half a century after this break. It came to an end when Sindh was conquered by the English during the final stage of a process which had started with the arrival of Europeans on the Indian coasts.

The Gamic era (a term coming from the name of Vasco da Gama) began in 1498 when the Portuguese reached India by sea. European sailors had started exploring the world to reach India and China and trade with them without paying the custom duties imposed by the Turkish Empire. The profits realized by Vasco da

Gama amounted to 60 times his investments. The discoveries made by Christopher Columbus favoured this long distance trade: America was easily conquered because her great civilizations of astronomers, architects and road builders could not vie with the armours, swords, horses, guns and cannons of the invaders and the gold and the silver of the New World, often redistributed between Europeans by Spanish orders to other countries (Holland for instance) or by the attacks of English pirates, were used to trade with India, China, Persia and Indonesia. Black slaves were brought from Africa to work in America and master this huge continent.

Western Europe soon dominated the oceans and created the first world economy. The merchants of Spain, Holland, France and England threw a net on the other continents. Very soon the manufactures of India were working in connection to the State, the aristocracy and the trade with Western powers that also created their own manufactures.[9] Gandhi is therefore absolutely right to say that the colonial conquerors were eagerly courted by the Indian States and rulers. The English Company finally prevailed: as an island, Britain saw all European wars as colonial wars and when the British Isles reached a state where they had to provide goods for America, Asia and Africa this tiny nation that was called England could only respond to the demands created by its colonial conquests and the destruction of the productive forces that already existed in these colonies or dominated countries, by starting an industrial revolution in the late eighteenth century and the early nineteenth century. The United Kingdom became the main world power for a century and a half and India was the pearl of the English Empire.

For India the Western shock came first with regional revolts against the Mughal centre in order to benefit directly from the world trade that the boats from Europe had mastered. These traders were greedy because their nations were hungry for spices, textiles and luxury goods which were not available on the cold and harsh continent and whenever they struck a deal the handshake very often would go as far as the elbow: The Western beggars often turned

---

[9]   H.T. Sorley, *Shah Abdul Latif of Bhit*, Oxford University Press, London, 1940, pp 144–150.

into conquerors! The English East Indian Company even became the tax collector of Mughal Emperors who had stopped (after Aurangzeb) traveling on horseback to administer and defend the various parts of their Empire. The divided Indian states were conquered one by one by the money or the armies of this powerful Company. This decay had already appeared clearly to traumatized Muslim scholars when Nadir Shah of Persia plundered Delhi (1739) and stole the prestigious Peacock Throne. The conqueror ruled Sindh for a decade. Nadir Shah's successors were not as successful and they lost Afghanistan to a Pashtun Dynasty, the Durrani. A few years later the Marathi reached Delhi, conquered it and left it. The depressed Muslim scholars reacted to these traumatic events by a conservative regress that tended to erase the Islamic centuries of philosophical and scientific creativity. Shah Waliullah Delhawi stressed the importance of law and obedience. The historical disasters of this difficult period could only be understood as a punishment from the Almighty angry against sins and disobedience. Slowly this very conventional trend became more important. Some scholars went as far as making research, rationality, justice and love appear as secondary factors of the faith.

However, Islam could still produce great rulers. In 1799, in Southern India, the son of Hyder Ali of Mysore, Tipu Sultan, a member of the Jacobine Club of revolutionary France, was killed during the storming of his capital by the troops of the English Company. Hyder and Tipu had challenged for many years the conquerors and modernized Mysore. Later the foreign invaders crushed the Marathi forces. Napier conquered Sindh (1843) against the heroic black general Hosh Muhammad and proceeded further West against the Balochi people. The Sikhs of Punjab were defeated in 1848 when they tried to restore their power against the English Company. Afghanistan resisted courageously against three British aggressions. The Himalayas and Central Asia were the playgrounds of England and Russia in the confrontation called *"the Great Game"*. Large Mountainous parts of Eastern Persia and Afghanistan were ascribed to England according to the Goldsmith line for Baluchistan (South-Western part of Pakistan) in 1871 and the Durand line for the North-Eastern border of the English colony.

Both Baloch and Pashtun peoples found themselves divided by artificial border between the parts of India that are now Pakistan and Iran and Afghanistan.

The first War of Independence[10] was led by the aristocrats, the Sepoy mutineers and most colonized people of the subcontinent (1857–1858). Aristocrats were often displaced by the ruling English Company and their kingdoms taken if they had no direct heirs. Guilds and business people were victimized by colonial laws and custom duties which favoured English imports into India. Zamindars (rich and corrupt tax collectors appointed by the English) were buying lands and upsetting the traditional rural order. Taxes were so heavy that farmers were starving. Even the Indian soldiers of the Company (the Sepoys) saw their privileges threatened. The revolution was defeated by the British troops (composed of Pashtuns and Sikhs) that refused to follow the angry aristocracy and the mutiny of the Sepoys. The Muslims who had fought against the English were crushed by a repression that involved displacements from urban to rural zones and the richest of them became conservative feudal land owners whereas the Hindu elite was competing for administrative, commercial and industrial positions. The last Emperor of India had backed the War of Independence and he was removed from the position that his family had so gloriously held for three hundred years. The British government did not forgive the Company to have been so harsh with the Indians as to provoke this great national upheaval, the British state took over and Victoria became the empress of India.

The history of Islam in the space which was to become Pakistan shows that this religion, while being involved in a process of unification, has nevertheless kept alive a diversity coming from debates and even struggles among the Muslims, different levels and forms of development (tribal and communal verticality versus horizontality of classes within states) and cultural features coming

---

[10] This major event is often referred to as the Great Mutiny by mainly British historians and as the First War of Independence by Indian historians.

from many religious or ethnic minorities like the Hindus, the Christians (local and Europeans), the Arabs, the Persians, the Turks, the Afghans...

Colonization

Colonization, which started in Bengal in 1757 and spread all over India, was cruel and harsh. A self-confident and arrogant administration ruled the country and taxed mercilessly the farmers, provoking more and more famines. Local industries were stifled by heavy custom duties in England and replaced in India by goods from Manchester. Colonial profits served the ambitions of the imperialist bourgeoisie and were used as crumbs to distribute to a working-class aristocracy who, therefore, became less revolutionary and gradually accepted capitalism. Colonization was a process of externalization of the colonized economy as it worked mainly in favour of the colonial masters and the colonizing country. This domination was subsequently an underdevelopment process: when Bengal was conquered (1757), India was still the second economic world power behind China. It represented then 18–20 % of the world economy, but after a century and a half of colonial rule, in 1947, when India and Pakistan became independent, both of them together only represented 4 or 5 % of the world economy, far from the United States, Britain and the USSR, much less than most individual Western countries.

Neither the Islamic pre-colonial order nor the Islam shaped by the colonial experience were deprived of diversity. Still nowadays the Barelvis majority (mild form of Sufism), the Deobandis (a strong purist school born as a reaction against colonization), the Ahl al Hadilla (Salafists) and Wahabis (a conservative trend from Arabia), the Pashtunwali (the Pashtun code of values and conduct) which is still very strong, the local pilgrimages and Saints make the Sunnite majority a patchwork of identities. Not all the Muslim citizens of the country see Pakistan as a true Islamic state. The Shi'ites (10 to 20 %) are divided into trends that are themselves subdivided. Dardic tribal groups like the Kalash animists, whose creed is mixed with proto-Hindu beliefs, have survived. Ahmadism (created by

Mizra Ghulam Ahmed, the Islamic Messiah, around 1897) derives from Islam but has been declared non-Muslim as the founder's title of Messiah, his being a reincarnation of Jesus, his identity with the Mahdi of the End of history and the function of many other prophets to come were seen as clear rejections of the Muslim proclamation that Muhammad was the last Prophet. Hindus, Sikhs, Jews, Christians, Zoroastrians haven't all left Pakistan during the dramatic partition of Pakistan and India.

Against colonization the inhabitants of this new nation have retained or altered many of their cultural features. They have redefined Urdu as the common language of Pakistan and the great medium of Muslim culture. Urdu then stood in opposition to Hindi, the very similar language which was to become the national tongue of India. Intellectuals and activists became nationalists, Pan-Islamists, liberals, trade-unionists, third-world militants and socialists (affiliated to Labourism or Marxism). They adopted or rejected non-violence, secularism, modernity and the calls from other peoples of the world. Diversity is still very much alive in Pakistan.

Islam is not only a militant cause but also, through one of its many hues, a way of life whose features can be tolerant and sensual. It would really be unfair to forget that, apart from a puritan or martial version of life, it is also a hedonistic way of life. Fed by the poems of Omar Khayyam praising the wine of the mystics or of the libertines, those of Ghalib whose lyric and mystic qualities seem to flow in the same river, the splendour of the ghazals (a most popular poetic form), the sensuality of dancing courtesans and the bewitching voices of singers, a very different world of idle lovers, refined courtesans and rich patrons has grown. The prodigal son may be a sinner but he is also a better man than his brother who is blinded by his arrogant certainty that he is a moral person. It is not impossible that some Muslims were exploring an Islamic equivalent of Tantra or the left-hand of Hinduism which was based on the idea that doing what's prohibited could be a way of discovering God. Human desire and its many and changing objects might help the believer to recognize the Object of all desires, God: the multiples of the totality feel desires that are obviously instrumental in the quest of the searching souls for the One. Ahmed Ali's sensual novel *Ocean of Night* [11] comes from this way of life that has created a hedonistic culture where desire, poetry and love celebrate life and beauty to challenge stern and hypocritical social conventions. Borders that judge, discriminate, condemn and reject the sinner may not be what God wishes most from his creatures and the faithful. Ignoring this paradoxical trend would be ignoring one of the cultures that made Pakistan what it still is even if some dogmatic and puritan believers don't want to accept this idea.

Therefore, to recognize all these trends requires qualities which cannot be accepted by a narrow vision of the nation that defined itself as the nation of the pure. Too many people in this country as well as in the whole world associate purity with strict rules that most often kill life. Such sad visions come from cruel historical experiences that left people devastated and traumatized. Colonialism is one of them. After 1857, the Muslims of India discovered that they were ostracized from progress, pushed into archaic forms of life, sent to rural areas far from the forces of renewal. The divide and rule game of the British turned them into a segregated community. They were treated like foreigners in their own country. The colonial ideologies pretended that what they call Islamic invasions from abroad had made India backward and that it was the duty of colonization to favour the real sons and would-be leaders of the land, the high-caste Hindus. The Muslims were only a martial community bound to serve a state. In no way could they rule it. Of course true nationalists, Hindus or Muslims, did not agree but some militants for home rule or even Independence, like Tilak from the Indian National Congress, used in the late nineteenth century and the early twentieth, Hindu festivals as a strategic moment to rehabilitate the colonized and defend national claims, which left many Muslims with the feeling that Indian Independence in a state dominated by the Hindu majority would not give them the recognition that they were entitled to receive.

This fear was to give birth to Pakistan.

---

[11] Ahmed Ali, *Ocean of Night*, Hind, Delhi, 1972. (1964)

According to some Muslims who were overcome by their anxiety about the future, decay could only be checked if the community restored her past values or, which is perhaps more accurate, the values that some intellectuals presented as the basic features of the creed. This position could prevent the faithful to trust the attitude that once made them great: a creativity which was the virtue that challenges history and adjusts the faith to disturbing changes. Such a reactive logic is not only the cause of the weakening of creativity, it tends to simplify world visions. As a consequence, huge contradictory ideological blocks were invoked (Muslims / Hindus, Sunnites / Shi'ites, true Muslims / hypocritical believers...) whereas reality is much more complex and open. Colonization had used this dangerous strategy for 150 years, opposing the Aryan Hindu cousins of the British Aryans to the Semitic and Mughal Islamic races and cults. Too many Indians, in the territories that were to become India and Pakistan, were eager to think along such dangerous lines. Colonization had produced too many humiliated identities looking for a scapegoat and ready to despise their brothers. Fears create such binary visions of the world and hatreds can unite people more easily than love. The opposition between a neurotic trend and a creative one is by no way a Muslim feature; it exists in all religions. It is a temptation that all believers should fear more than other creeds.

On the whole we must say that the poor electoral results of the fanatical parties show that Pakistani people have resisted the temptation but the danger that such groups represent nevertheless exists and makes everyday life as much as national life difficult for the population of the country. The diversity of Pakistan requires a strategy inspired from the old Urs festivals and an open and creative leadership able to bring about open solutions to real problems. Such a trend of leaders cannot easily find its way in such a tense and divided situation full of anxieties and resentment. As a consequence, leaders have often been cautious and too conventional. Without a creative open national trend most regions defended their interests that often prevailed on the transformation of the nation as a whole. Even before the country was born, these questions haunted the minds of some of the people who saw Pakistan as a great hope. Spinoza says that hope is a sad passion as it makes what is not yet real prevail on what is already real, whereas joyful passions grow on the rich soil of present human solidarities. Therefore, the future may be a very deceptive dream.

Who were the founders of Pakistan and what were their motives?

CHAPTER II: THE FOUNDING FATHERS OF PAKISTAN

It is a truism to claim that the British conquest of India and its detrimental impact on the Indian Muslims threw the members of this community into a state of consternation and hopelessness. Whereas for the Hindus the arrival of the British was simply seen as a foreign ruler replacing another, for the Muslims it meant a reversal of their fortunes and privileged position in the subcontinent. Seeing power slipping out of their hands, it was, as a matter of fact, a too harsh reality for them to come to terms with. This new condition made them withdraw in despair and attempts at ant-colonial struggle, besides being limited, were all doomed to failure. The Faraizi Movement, for instance, which was initiated by Haji Shariat Allah in the Bengal region in the first half of the nineteenth century, is a good example illustrating a Muslim uprising manifesting itself as anti-British. Yet, the large-scale demonstration of Muslim rejection of the new status quo was unquestionably the happenings of 1857. This 'Great Mutiny', as British historians tend to downgrade it, was a moment when Muslims and Hindus joined hands in an effort to throw the yoke of British colonialism. It started as an upsurge in the barracks conducted by a group of malcontent sepoys, or native soldiers in the service of the British East India Company, spontaneously reacting to some kind of dissatisfaction and grievances. Within a short period of time, this mutiny snowballed and turned into a popular uprising as the civilian population throughout the north of India joined the movement. Nevertheless, the British quickly quelled this revolt thanks to a number of factors, important among which being disunity and lack of coordination among the insurgents, due in the main to the existence of divergent — and sometimes opposed — objectives among them.
Following the failure of this bloody event, the Indian Muslims plunged further into despondency. Their situation went from bad to worse in the aftermath of the hostilities, especially that the British officials decided to designate them as the only culprits responsible

for the outbreak of the uprising as well as the ensuing atrocities that were committed by the rebels against the European residents. Accordingly, they were to be subjected to a discriminatory policy that disfavoured them in every walk of life. By all accounts, this vindictive attitude on the part of the British wreaked havoc on the whole Muslim community, which was reduced to a state of degradation and misery. The following passage, addressed in the wake of the revolt by the Muslim community of Delhi to Governor-General Charles Canning, reflected their predicament:

> We the Muslim inhabitants of Delhi have since sustained the extreme losses of life, property and honour. At present we have absolutely nothing to feed our children and ourselves. There is no ceiling under which we could seek shelter against inclement weather, and no clothings (sic) to cover our bodies. Thousands of us not bearing the severities of climate perished last year and if nothing is done to protect us many more will die this season.[12]

Apart from the limited scenes of anti-colonial violence, Indian Muslims' expression of rejection of British rule took the form of adopting a passive attitude towards the new establishment, looking at the foreign masters with a mixture of distrust and suspicion. This negative reaction was characterized by their avoiding contact with anything associated with the British, including their culture and education. It is worth digressing at this point to mention the fact that this anti-western attitude was enthusiastically encouraged by the traditional *ulama,* or the orthodox religious scholars, who, for various reasons, struggled to convince the Muslim minds of the incompatibility between the tenets of Islam and western culture.[13] Towards this end, they exhorted the members of their community to keep away from British schools, which they referred to as "abodes of ignorance".[14]

---

[12] Punjab, *C.S. Records*, General Department of proceedings of the 1st January, 1859, F. N° 11–12. Quoted by Syed Razi Wasti, 'British Policy towards the Indian Muslims Immediately after 1857', S. R. Wasti (ed.), Renaissance Publishing House, Delhi, 1993 (1–24), p. 22.

[13] Mian M. Sharif, *A History of Muslim Philosophy: With Short Accounts of Other Disciplines and the Modern Renaissance in Muslim Lands* (Vol II), Otto Harrassowitz, Wiesbaden, Germany, 1966, p. 1589.

[14] Rajmohan Gandhi, *Understanding the Muslim Mind*, Penguin Books India, New Delhi, 1987, p. 21.

In a word, the post-1857 era was qualified by historians and contemporaries as the darkest chapter in the historical process of the Indian Muslims who, with their back to the wall, faced a serious multi-dimensional challenge to their very existence as a minority in the subcontinent. This new context would serve as a catalyst that prompted the members of this community to think of themselves as a separate group distinct from the rest of the inhabitants of India, a line of thought that would eventually culminate in the creation in 1947 of the first independent Muslim nation in South Asia, Pakistan. However, this outcome could perhaps never have happened without the intervention of three prominent Indian Muslim personalities: Sir Sayyid Ahmad Khan (1817–1898), Muhammad Iqbal (1876–1938) and Muhammad Ali Jinnah (1876–1948).

Sayyid Ahmad Khan

It was against the gloomy backdrop described in the paragraphs above that Sir Sayyid Ahmad Khan (the title 'Sir' was conferred to him by the British at a later stage of his life) decided to step into the limelight on the Indian stage. Having witnessed the sufferings of his coreligionists, he felt duty-bound to devote his time and energy to saving them. At the height of the bloody events, he had once contemplated leaving for Egypt fleeing the turmoil at home; however, he soon changed his mind and decided to remain in India in order to take matters into his own hands. Actually, this change of mind occurred to Sayyid Ahmad Khan upon his visit in 1858 to the city of Moradabad, one of the hotspots of the uprising, where he was moved by the plight of his fellow Muslims. Hafeez Malik quoted him personally describing the emotions that engulfed him at that moment:

> When I came to Moradabad...which was in fact a big house of mourning for the death and destruction of our nation's well-to-do families — my grief was deepened. Then and there it occurred to me that my personal flight to a place of safety was contrary to all feelings of compassion and manhood. No, I must share the troubles of my nation; and whatever the afflictions there might be I must help to alleviate them. This is a national obligation. Then I

decided not to leave the country, and dedicated myself to the national cause.¹⁵

If there was anything that Sayyid Ahmad Khan was convinced about, it is the fact that the fateful happenings of 1857 had delivered a coup de grace to the already staggering Muslim community in South Asia. In such circumstances, he believed, mourning one's lost glory was to no avail; instead, it was time for the Muslims of India to courageously face up to their new reality and make some sacrifices as the only way forward.

Therefore, as a precondition for a new departure for the whole community, Sayyid Ahmad Khan deemed it necessary to, on the one hand, clear the misunderstanding that characterized relations between his coreligionists and the British, and on the other, 'brighten' their (Muslims') image in the eyes of the foreign masters, hitherto seen as *bêtes noires* in the subcontinent. With this objective in mind, and as a first step, he wrote, in 1859 and 1860, two pamphlets entitled *Asbab-i Baghawat-i Hind* (Essay on the causes of the Indian Revolt) and the *Loyal Muhammedans of India*. Regarding *Asbab-i Baghawat-i Hind*, he intended it to serve as an apologia for those 'few' Muslims who had committed a 'serious' blunder by rebelling against Her Majesty's Government in India, but also sought through it to vindicate the members of the Muslim community of the exclusive responsibility for the revolt.

In *The Loyal Muhammedans of India*, which was intended as a follow-up to the previous pamphlet, Sayyid Ahmad Khan's main objective was to shed light on the many instances of support that some Indian Muslims offered to the British in their effort to regain control in the rebellion-affected areas. While lambasting those involved in the bloodshed, whose misbehaviour he held "in utter abhorrence, as being in the highest degree criminal, and wholly inexcusable,"¹⁶ he also insisted on the fact that the colonial government should praise those who stood by it during those difficult times. It

---

[15] Hafeez Malik, *Sir Sayyid Ahmad Khan and Muslim Modernization in India and Pakistan*, Columbia University Press, New York, 1980, p. 77.

[16] Anil C. Banerjee, *Two Nations: The Philosophy of Muslim Nationalism*, Concept Publishing Company, New Delhi, 1981, pp. 82–83.

is interesting to note that in an extraordinary show of support, this Muslim leader himself took the risk of securing a safe passage for British residents who were held hostage by the insurgents in a section of the town of Bijnor.

In the meantime, after gauging the conditions in the subcontinent, Sayyid Ahmad Khan realized the urgent need to come up with an elaborate plan to modernize as well as energize the hitherto comatose Muslim community. This was fulfilled through the launching of a vigorous reformist movement, historically known as the Aligarh Movement, which affected every aspect of Muslim life. This overarching approach was intended by the reform-minded Ahmad Khan to bring the Indian Muslims face to face with the hurdles that kept them lagging far behind the rest of Indians, and accordingly, all kinds of topics were to be dealt with, which ranged from those of major importance, such as interfaith relations, to petty issues related to everyday life, such as table manners. Three main themes were to underlie Sayyid Ahmad Khan's reformist agenda: first, loyalty to the British and aloofness from politics; second, devotion to education; and third, socio-religious reform.

With regard to the first theme, Sayyid Ahmad Khan resorted to the principle of realpolitik by advising his co-religionists to give politics a wide berth and urging them to adopt a loyalist attitude towards the British since they were, to quote Jim Masselos, the "patrons par excellence" in the country who "were responsible for distributing the limited quantity of 'loaves and fishes' available."[17] This explains why he vehemently opposed the Indian National Congress, founded in 1885, and warned his fellow Muslims against joining it. Actually, he regarded this political organization as too 'disrespectful' to the British and that it was in the interest of the Muslims to keep being on good terms with the foreign rulers. Besides that, Sayyid Ahmad Khan feared that his community would be overwhelmed by the Hindu majority if one day the British decided to leave India. This line of thought would later on be taken up by his successors who would use that 'feeling of insecurity' as a

---

[17] Jim Masselos, *Indian Nationalism: An History*, Sterling Publishers Private Limited, New Delhi, 1996, p. 120.

key argument in their quest for a separate nation for the Indian Muslims.

Sayyid Ahmad Khan's philosophy of loyalism to the foreign rulers was not only driven by his opportunism and realistic pragmatism but also by conviction. As an 'Occidentalist' who admired and idealized the British and their civilization, he saw nothing wrong in having the Indian Muslims get closer to them and pledge allegiance to them. As he put it: "God has made them rulers over us. Our Prophet has said that if God places over you a black negro slave as ruler you must obey him."[18] After all, as he often emphasized, the Muslims had much more in common with the monotheism of Christianity than the polytheism of Hinduism. Accordingly, his efforts were focused on the delineation of the many similarities that existed between the two Abrahamic faiths. P. Spear stated that Sayyid Ahmad Khan always underscored the "fundamental Islamic and Christian ideas with their common Judaic heritage."[19]

In the meantime, the adoption of loyalism towards the British rulers, in Sayyid Ahmad Khan's view, was not enough to bring about a genuine rehabilitation of the hitherto downtrodden Muslim community. He realized the fact that the major stumbling block facing the Muslims was the total absence of modern education. Hence, the next significant point in his programme was education. According to Khursheed K. Aziz, Sayyid Ahmad Khan's slogan was "devote yourselves to education; this is your only salvation."[20]

Therefore, in this regard, he launched a country-wide campaign to help raise funds in order to set up a Muslim college. This was fulfilled by 1875, when the Muhammadan Anglo-Oriental College (also known as the Aligarh College) was founded where both Islamic and Western studies were to be offered. Actually, the aim of this educational project was to allow the Muslim youth to imbibe western culture and sciences without causing any damage to their

---

[18] Quoted in, Shan Muhammad, *Writings and Speeches of Sir Syed Ahmad Khan*, Nachiketa Publications Limited, Bombay, 1972, p. 193.
[19] Percival Spear, *A History of India: From the Sixteenth Century to the Twentieth Century*, Penguin Books, Middlesex, 1990, p. 225.
[20] Khursheed K. Aziz, *The Making of Pakistan: A Study in Nationalism*, Chattos & Windus, London, 1967, p. 20.

Islamic upbringing; that is, creating a modernized Muslim generation who, in the words of Karen Armstrong, "without becoming carbon-copies of the British," would retain "a sense of their own cultural identity."[21]

On the other hand, Sayyid Ahmad Khan was convinced that the only panacea for the ills and sufferings of his coreligionists lay in their adoption of a more liberal and broad-minded approach to their faith as well as to their social relations in the Indian multi-cultural environment. Such openness would unquestionably help them overcome their religious prejudice which, in his opinion, had so far served as a barrier that hindered their progress. This prompted him to embark on a large-scale socio-religious reformist campaign among the community, which took the form of launching a journal entitled *Tehzib-ul-Akhlaq*, that is, 'Refinement of Morals or Social Reformer'. Viewed with suspicious eyes by the more orthodox elements of the Muslim community, this pamphlet, which was published in Urdu, set as an objective the development of the moral standards of the Indian Muslims to, as described by Muhammad Y. Abbasi, the "highest degree of civilization," and to effect a "fundamental religious, moral and social reform."[22] In doing so, Sayyid Ahmad Khan challenged some of the long-established social norms — sustained by the traditional *ulama* for centuries — by filling the pages of *Tehzib-ul-Akhlaq* with articles where he levelled heavy criticisms at the 'old-fashioned' and 'disgusting' customs, which were at that time rampant among the Muslims of India. In a word, he wanted to rid his coreligionists of their various misconceptions and purify them of the many un-Islamic folkways and superstitions which held them back.

In a nutshell, Sayyid Ahmad Khan's reformist agenda was based on a new approach which was liberalist both in form and content, unlike any of the previous reformist movements that Muslim South Asian history had ever recorded which, on the whole,

---

[21] Karen Armstrong, *Islam: A Short History*, Phoenix, London, 2000, p. 128.
[22] Muhammad Y. Abbasi, *The Genesis of Muslim Fundamentalism in British India*, Eastern Book Corporation, New Delhi, 1987, p. 21.

tended to be more conservative and reactionary in character.²³ He used his numerous interventions and writings as a means to inculcate into the minds of the Muslims the desire to embrace a new pattern of life which would be adjustable to the new demands of the time while remaining Islamic in roots. For instance, he held the view that the Islamic faith and Western liberalism could go hand in hand since the Holy Quran was in perfect conformity with the natural laws that were being discovered by modern sciences. In this respect, he warned his coreligionists against *taqlid*, that is, blind imitation of old interpretations of the scriptures (i.e., Quran and the *Hadith* or the Prophetic sayings), and encouraged them, instead, to commit themselves to *ijtihad*, that is, independent reinterpretation of these religious texts, in the light of modern times. In reference to Sayyid Ahmad Khan, the famous Urdu poet who turned into a national leader of the Muslims, Iqbal, once said that he was: "the first Indian Muslim to react to the modern age."²⁴

Sayyid Ahmad Khan's preaching of liberalist ideas among his community incurred him a great deal of anger from the orthodox religious scholars, who accused him of apostasy and dubbed him as a "kafir", meaning an infidel. Be that as it may, a significant section of Indian Muslims joined his movement and, more or less, stuck by his recommendations, even after he passed away in 1898 — though with slight changes in accordance with the evolution of the political situation in British India.

Before ending this section on Sayyid Ahmad Khan, it is important to note that despite being well aware of the fact that there was a huge conflict of interest between the Indian Muslims and their Hindu fellow countrymen, Sayyid Ahmad Khan had never been opposed to the idea of having both communities coexist peacefully and share the same land and a common destiny. In fact, he was in favour of fraternal relations between both communities

---

[23] The best-known Muslim reformist movement was the one led by Shah Walyi Allah Delhavi (1703–1762). For more information about this topic, see Belkacem Belmekki, "Shah Walyi Allah Delhavi's Attempts at Religious Revivalism in South Asia", in *Anthropos: International Review of Anthropology and Linguistics*, N° 109/2, Anthropos Institut, Germany, 2014 (pp. 621–625).

[24] Rajmohan Gandhi, op. cit., p. 43.

which he often referred to as the two eyes on the beautiful face of India. Yet, this disposition was going to change due to the increasing anti-Muslim activism among some Hindu zealots in the decades following the revolt, demonstrated through incidents such as the Urdu-Hindi language controversy or the campaign to ban the slaughtering of cows. These acts affected Sayyid Ahmad Khan's views regarding the future of his community. As he put it:

> Now I am convinced that both these communities will not join wholeheartedly in anything .... On account of the so-called "educated" people, hostility between the two communities will increase immensely in the future. He who lives will see.[25]

In the post-Sayyid Ahmad Khan's era, new developments in British India were to compel his followers to take a different course of action whereby they could no longer afford to abide by his key commandment regarding political disengagement, — though still remaining loyal subjects of Her/His Majesty.

Amid the turmoil that the subcontinent was engulfed in during the first decades of the twentieth century, there emerged another Muslim figure, Muhammad Iqbal, who, like his predecessor Sayyid Ahmad Khan, distinguished himself in the defence of the Muslim cause in British India.

Muhammad Iqbal: the Dream of Pakistan and the Islamic Renaissance

Muhammad Iqbal was born in 1877 in Punjab. His family was rich and cultured. Pakistani intellectuals often connect his poetical works to the birth of Pakistan, which is legitimate, but these interpretations should not be stressed at the expense of the full meaning of Iqbal's literary, philosophical and theological works. Many critics and readers are either not fully aware of the deeper meaning of his writings or they try to avoid the most disturbing aspects of a very original thought that frightens them and does not fit into the conservative reality that they favour in Pakistan.

---

[25] Quoted in, ibid., p. 27.

Iqbal's ancestors were Brahmins. They belonged to the highest caste in Hinduism, venerated for the purity of its members, their superior karma, priestly responsibilities and prestigious Sanskrit culture. They had converted to Islam. In Punjab, the part of India where he grew as a child, Sikhs, Hindu, Muslims had lived together for centuries. Gandhi often said that peace is not recorded by historical chronicles, only fighting and wars feed the books written by historians, so that we are not fully aware of the very old and refined Indian ability of dealing peacefully with other creeds, cultures and ethnic groups. The three main religions of Punjab shared a common culture in spite of their various backgrounds. The Urdu language unified them. Poetry was venerated. Iqbal also spoke fluently Persian, the language of kings in India and the medium of Persian culture and the Sufi poets of Iran.

In 1895 he went to Lahore, the pearl of Urdu culture, as a student of the University. Later he joined Trinity College in Cambridge, visited Germany, the land of philosophers and the cradle of philosophical systems that dominated the cultural life and creativity of the Western world. The West was at its climax in the late nineteenth century. It seemed then that Western civilization dominated all continents and pushed aside other cultures to a secondary rank or even erased them. The West appeared as the result of human progress, the creation of a past opening on a future that Western sciences, technologies and armies carved. For most Europeans (and North-Americans), science was Western science and no other cognitive system could vie with it. The United Kingdom, thanks to its huge Empire whose pearl was India, was the main superpower of the nineteenth century.

By 1895, nevertheless, Germany had appeared as a rival for England and in the East Japan hoped to develop as a strong and prosperous industrial power and wanted to be the liberator of subdued Asia. Since the industrial revolution, technology had progressed so much that the Western powers were suddenly unable to sell the goods that they produced to a narrow national market and colonization appeared as the solution to this crisis which they overcame by conquering territories that gave them cheap raw materials and new markets, especially captive markets. The industrialized world appeared in 1895 aggressive, imperialistic and incredibly hard. For the dominated continents this arrogant and successful civilization was both fascinating and frightening. The discovery of the West as a leading cultural, industrial and military power was a shock for the young man, Iqbal, who was so proud of his Urdu culture, but his reaction was original in so far as he wanted to absorb in his vision both the East and the West by reconciling the positive features of each and reaching a common horizon beyond their weaknesses. His rehabilitation of his culture became for him a universal issue.

The desire to rehabilitate a dominated culture is quite common. Japanese, Chinese, Arabs, South Americans and Africans have tried to create new relations with the West by adopting some of its ways and reassessing their culture. The Islamic world was of course part of this attempt. The Traditionalists wanted to reassess their Islamic, spiritual and moral culture and they saw the West as a threat for the everlasting values of their religion. They only accepted from the brave new world its technology and tried to preserve their beloved past as a sacred relic. The Liberals of the colonized élite, fascinated by the modern world imposed by the White imperialists, wanted to adopt the western model and they criticized their own religions as backward cultures responsible for the inferior development of the East (Asia) and the South (Africa and South America). In other words, the Traditionalists confirmed the Western view that their culture was rigid, nostalgic of the past and that it was a threat to modern ideas and ways, while the Liberals confirmed the superiority of the West and saw their own culture with the eyes of the Westerners as the cause of the backwardness of the non-European cultures. Sometimes the westernized élite of the dominated countries is tempted by Marxist ideas but then the progressive intellectuals come to share many of the prejudices of the Liberals: the future is inspired by the West (a Promethean vision of the future based on democratic aspirations to equality, human rights, industrialization, high standards of living…) whereas religion is for them a trap or an opium to be left aside. Iqbal was original because he wanted to be fully modern and fully Islamic. He intended, as a modern man, to reopen the road of human progress that was checked in the West by violence, narrow-mindedness and rejection of God and, as a Muslim, to revive the Koranic vision of the future that had often been stifled by a repetitive and uncreative reading of the sacred texts of Islam. For Iqbal one cannot bring modernity to its end without the prophetic forces of religion (Islam) and one cannot be a Muslim without opening the old religious ways to the revival brought by the creative forces that the West has woken up in the fields of culture, science and technology. His position avoids the traps set by Western hegemony, religious conservatism and the Liberals' blind admiration of the West.

In the past the struggle against the forces of the establishment backed by the conservative *ulama* took several roads that Iqbal followed in spite of the fact that for some thinkers they were to be avoided.

In Bagdad the Mutazilites and Al-Kindi (the author of the *Virtuous City*) took the path of rationality and experiments to overcome the tendency to establish the truth by quoting old texts in endless passive comments and venerating traditions and conventions. First the rationalists were favoured by the Abbasid power but this bold trend frightened rulers whose enlightenment was declining as the ruling classes were becoming more rigid and their interests more entrenched in conservative social and political positions. The reaction against the rationalists went along with decay and division: soon the Abbasid Empire split into many rival states.

Against the Almoravids who had dominated the West of the Muslim world, the rising Almohads, encouraged by Ibn Tumart, favoured a school of rationalists that Ibn Hazm and Averroes made famous.[26] The first one revived Zahirist theories that state that a textual statement is useless unless backed by a strong reasoning or an experiment. Averroes commented in depth the works of Aristotle and set the path of reason for the future. Unfortunately, this attempt came to an end with the decay of the Almohades defeated by the Spanish *reconquista* at Las Navas de Tolosa in 1212.

---

[26] Mohamed Abed al-Jabi, *Introduction à la critique de la pensée arabe*, Découverte, Paris, 1994.

The Sufi thought and experience in Islam can be divided into a conventional trend and a non-conventional one that produced mystics like Al-Hallaj, Rumi, Abd el-Kader whose visions and lives enlightened Islam. In India converts to Islam were most often people moved by saints, poets and musicians. This trend has obviously influenced Iqbal. During his stay in the West, he met the French researcher, Louis Massignon, who had written a famous thesis on Al-Hallaj and was himself a Sufi.

These historical rationalist or mystical experiences helped Iqbal to base his thought on the hope of a necessary Islamic Renaissance. Already the Arabs had launched their Renaissance (The *Nada*) that studied, among many themes, the relation of Islam to the modern world.

From Germany Iqbal retained the stormy thought of Nietzsche. He wanted to capture the *Zeitgeist* of the West, *modernity* and the *kairos* of his time. From France he retained the works of Bergson, a philosopher who saw the growth of humanity as a rich and fruitful contradiction between rigid rational organization and mystic inspiration. The first trend organizes society and the second anticipates its necessary change to reach a higher stage. When the call of a hero (Buddha, Jesus, Jeremy, Isaïa, Muhammad, Al-Halaj, Rumi, Kabir…) and his vision come to prevail in men's hearts and heads, humanity is ready to reach a new level of moral and spiritual development. Therefore, a new organization of life appears but it is bound to be opposed by new prophets and dreamers of an even higher future. This process is infinite and it comes to connect both the human and the divine. In the early twentieth century Iqbal could also read the works of Aurobindo Ghosh, a Hindu and Bengali mystic who thought that spiritual and mental forces would ultimately take over and rule the cosmos. According to recent scientific discoveries, the experiment by itself determines its result, for instance the movement of particles. It is therefore legitimate to think that the scientist's intention (his mental) is an important factor, which shows that the mental can rule matter if it reaches a higher level that might come in the future thanks to human new evolutionary developments. Iqbal's vision of evolution is partly indebted to the Bengali mystic who settled near Chennai and Pondicherry and whose writings he could not ignore.[27]

Back home, Iqbal deepened his intuitions as a poet and summed them up in his *Reconstruction of the Thought of Islam*. He revealed his burning desire to see the rebirth of Islam when he praised the policy of Ata Turk in Turkey and when, very often, he insisted on the concept *of Ijtihad*, the intellectual creative effort to settle problematic or controversial issues. In 1930, at a meeting of the Muslim League of India, he expressed his desire to see the regions populated by a majority of Muslims in the North-West of India form an independent entity. This part of colonial India was to become first Western Pakistan and finally Pakistan after the break with the Eastern component that became independent under the name of Bangladesh. As an intellectual and a poet, he thought of this Islamic union as a mostly spiritual reality but this stance was anyway to make him one of the founding fathers of Pakistan. For sometimes Jinnah, who was to become the Governor of independent Pakistan, courted Iqbal and they very often met. Iqbal died in 1938, almost a decade before the birth of the country he imagined and where, perhaps, he would have like to see the flowering of the Islamic Renaissance he wished so much in order to revive his religion, enlighten the West and offer a new scope of development and fulfilment to the world and humanity.

Three stages sum up Iqbal's thought:

The understanding of the present time (*Zeitgeist*). He experienced the very disturbing reality of the West as a shock but not as a trauma. A shock is to produce a relevant response. It is a cruel but necessary and positive experience. It makes people wake up and cope with reality. On the contrary, a traumatism destroys the victim to the point that he / she becomes unable to cope with the situation.

---

[27] Iqbal lived before Theillard de Chardin. No one can deny that he would have been most interested in the French and Catholic scientist's vision of evolution. According to Theillard de Chardin, as complexity of organic structures raises thought, the growing world is more and more unified in thought and organization in a spiritual process led by God with the help of man.

What has been experienced is beyond the acceptable and so it is deprived of an adequate language to be integrated to the emotions, the soul and the body of the victim. Instead of recovering, he / she gets caught in a repetitive attitude that unconsciously recreates the traumatic experience in order to come to terms with it. So, the victim of a trauma often goes from one disastrous experience to another and the possibility of integrating what happened to his / her thought and language is much more limited than in the case of a shock. Iqbal, as a man of words, a poet, as a person who met other great personalities of his time and exchanged ideas with them, was to find a way towards an Islamic Renaissance without retaining the darker part of the past and without falling into the traps set by the Western hegemony. He understood that rejecting Islam as a backward force was as wrong as hating blindly the West. So, his relation with western modernity went so far and so deep that he discovered its merits as well as its flaws. For him recent history had revealed, thanks to European science and rationality, that the human future was an endless creation but it had also revealed that it had also closed the shining way of the future by limiting progress to the production and exchange of material goods and an arrogant technological domination of nature. Such a dispensation only fed the human *ego* (from which comes the word egoistic) and a very poor teleology deprived of deep references to the Creator and the values of religions. What looked like a break in human history, the humanistic stance on man's creativity and power, was actually, according to Iqbal, a continuity when related to God's vision of the future, but the West was unable to see it because its modernity insists on *ex nihilo* creation on a world that is *tabula rasa* and leads to consumerism and chrematistic ways (the domination of finance) that lead to a dead-end. The lack of a higher dimension of life, history and evolution has reduced the once creative impulse of the Renaissance and Enlightenment in the West to a mortifying entity.

The Renaissance to come. Islam too, according to Iqbal, had lost the infinite creative impulse given by the Koran in the repetition of textual truths impoverished by conservative scholars and a tradition of interpretation of the text deprived of the creative vitality of life, history and evolution.[28] The Muslims, according to Iqbal, must understand what Creation is actually for the Quran: "*God is man's companion in his worldly task, provided man takes the initiative.*"[29] It is also obvious that God first called Abraham / Ibrahim to talk to him about an incredible and wonderful future. Iqbal himself showed the creative collaboration between God and Man in his poems when he told God in his collection of poems entitled *Eastern Message:* "*You created the night, I made the lamp.*"[30] For Iqbal, Islamic sacred texts endlessly try to bring the Muslims to accept that "*The earth will become Heaven*"[31] as the poet said in his *Songs of the Angel*. After all, according to Al-Jili: "*Nature is the crystallisation of a divine idea.*"[32] If the *ego* brought about in the West is unworthy of such a future, Islam, according to Iqbal must bring about a superior kind of *ego*, that he calls the *Ego*. The conception of man limited by a technology dedicated to hedonistic consumption, money, profit and power must be checked by an Islamic Renaissance dedicated to the freedom and creativity of man. Iqbal wants to replace the Western process of growing individualism by a process of individuation, which consists in developing in us infinite abilities. To the individual who pretends to be the only substance of history, he prefers the person who inhabits the world as God's creation. The believer will then become one with the rhythms of the world and he or she will open his / her soul to the creation's deeper purpose. Man must be defined not so much as a thinker (Iqbal criticized Descartes' Cogito: "*I think, therefore I am.*") but as an active subject. This forgotten message of the Koran and this forgotten dimension of Islam will, through a Muslim Renaissance, contribute to help the West to get out of the deadly trap where it is tempted to lose its soul and future.

The World to come. Rousseau believed in the human faculty of improvement and he wrote his famous novel entitled *La nouvelle Héloïse* to describe a community inspired by his heroin, Julie, to reach

---

[28] Abdennour Bider, *L'Islam face à la mort de Dieu*, François Bourin, Paris, 2010.
[29] Koran: XIII, 11.
[30] Bider, op. cit., p 139.
[31] Ibid., p 140.
[32] Ibid., p 147.

truth and love, social justice and moral perfection. Spinoza said that the soul can be attached to everlasting ideas that free her from the mortal world and tie her to immortality. Bergson has described the universe as "*a machine to create Gods.*"[33] He meant that the call of heroes produces higher spiritual humans who work with God. For Al Hallaj the mystic doesn't join God, he welcomes God in his life: God is therefore the One who comes into His creation to make it perfect, not the One whom human beings must join! So, the universe will open its material nature to Him in a process that will transform Man and nature. The Sharia then will become not a normative law but a free creative human nature committed to the whole world. Religion merges with creation for Iqbal. The Western dream of the domination of nature and time will be uplifted to be happy meeting between the creature and the Creator. The Eastern conception of Fate and submission to God has become a free and joyful meeting of God's freedom and man's free will. Sometimes Iqbal feels so sure that God is our desire and future that the word Time and the word God have the same meaning for him.

Was Iqbal the father of Pakistan? His ideas go much beyond the creation of a single new State. Nevertheless, Jinnah thought that Pakistan owed a lot to Iqbal. The poet's imagination gave birth to Jinnah's vision of a 'home for the Muslims of India'. Iqbal was influential to bring back Jinnah from his exile in England in the early thirties. He revived the Islamic cultural background of the leader of the Muslim League and inspired him so that the politician would turn the poet's intuitions into concrete claims. Bergson's vision of the importance of mystics in history perfectly fits what happened between Iqbal and Jinnah: the saints, artists and mystics first capture the imagination of their time and latter inspired disciples change these aspirations into concrete claims and actions which turn the dream into a rational project bound to lift humanity to a higher step of its evolution. Thanks to Iqbal Jinnah could forget daily political worries and dream of Pakistan as the land of the pure.

---

[33] Henri Bergson, *Les deux sources de la morale et de la religion*, PUF, Paris, 1958, p 338. (Our translation)

Of course, no one would see nowadays Pakistan as a higher level of life and civilization. Some people even call it a 'failed State' or a 'rogue State'! The fact is that Jinnah's dream, inspired by Iqbal, simultaneously succeeded to create Pakistan while failing to rise at the level of Iqbal's dreams. Politicians of course cannot fulfil dreams. They listen to them, recognize the beauty of their poetry, even venerate some of their ideas, but they have their own agenda, they are realistic and they cannot be dreamers. One could therefore dismiss Iqbal as a very bad politician but this negative position is not fair to the great intellectual, his experience, his generosity and his works as a poet and a thinker. He dreamed of Pakistan not as a politician and we must not forget that his vision concerned the whole world and all the Muslims, not only India and the North West of India. When a new nation is coming to birth, when it is only a protonation, people hope for the best and in their minds, it is more a Utopia than a concrete nation with a State, a constitution, a ruling class and citizens. This Utopia can lure the militants into submission to a new ruling class or work against the sordid interests that would kill the hopes of the people. In the case of Iqbal we cannot doubt that he wanted to inspire the people for the best. He still remains one of the few whose words can bring Pakistan out of the deceptive path chosen by feudal landowners, merchants, soldiers and politicians. Not only Pakistan but the whole world!

Actually, Iqbal's effort to be one with his time, one with God and the rhythms of creation, was not the dream of an isolated idealist unable to cope with the real world. Bergson wanted Man to be one with time and its rhythms when he defined duration as the time of the soul, freed from organized and oppressive social space and time, and he saw in this relation between Man and Time (duration) the source of the mystic intuitions that first anticipate then carve the world to come. In Paris, when Bergson and Iqbal were alive, when Iqbal dreamed of an Indian North-Western Muslim entity, lived a young African intellectual, then a student, called Leopold Cedar Senghor, who was to adapt the romantic feelings towards nature to the African mind and the African rhythms in his artistic, critical, philosophical and political works. These ideas on the energies of the universe and their relations with personalities able to connect with them also developed in Spain with Ortega y Gasset and Maria Zambrano and of course in South America. Nowadays the Senegalese philosopher Suleyman Bachir Diagne, who insists on the connections between Bergson, Iqbal and Senghor, is a true disciple of these great thinkers as well as a true Muslim. It seems that Iqbal's soul was vibrating with the whole world, probably unconscious that his thoughts, poems and dreams were anticipating what was to become the Third World Revolution.

A dream cannot create a perfect nation but a nation that had no dreamers is very poor indeed. Pakistan still needs Iqbal. Of course, the one who led the Muslims to Pakistan was Jinnah. He was a practical man but, as a friend of the great poet, he knew that Iqbal's dreams were as necessary to the new nation as daily bread.

Muhammad Ali Jinnah

Muhammad Ali Jinnah was born in 1876 in Karachi in a rich family. He was the son of a lawyer. Karachi was the main city of Sindh that was part a province related to Bombay (Mumbai), the regional capital of the West of colonized India. In 1893 his family settled in Bombay. It was a cosmopolitan city inhabited by three great communities apart from the British colonial masters: the Hindus, the Muslims and the Parsees whose rich business families were already important in the Indian economy. Bombay's prosperous bourgeoisie had in the past made fortunes in the opium trade with China boosted by the English to balance their trade with the old Mandshu Empire. The Muslim population was very diverse too and Jinnah was a Muslim from the Shi'ite Ismaelian trend whose spiritual leader was the Aga Khan.

Muhammad Ali studied in Islamic and Christian institutions till a British friend of his father proposed him to take the young man to train him in business skills in England but instead, once in the United Kingdom, Jinnah decided to study Law at Lincoln's Inn. He said later that he chose this institution because he saw the name of Prophet Mohammad among the names of the world great legislators written on the front of Lincoln's Inn. Actually, what he saw was not the Prophet's name but a statue. Jinnah had to adapt this anecdote to the taste of Muslims who would be shocked by the representation of the Prophet. Conservatives and Liberals were the two Parties that ruled England and the young student was influenced by the Liberal thinkers of the United Kingdom. Jinnah admired the integrity of Gladstone, the grand old man of the Liberal Party, an enemy of colonial adventures and a believer in the virtues of peaceful trade. He read the works of Bentham, Mill, Spencer and even Auguste Comte, the French philosopher who is considered a one of the founders of a new scientific discipline: sociology. We can understand why Jinnah trusted the engineering of society by superior minds and disliked anarchy. Liberalism starts from the individual and his own free will and efforts. According to these ideas the less successful could at least take advantage of the trickling down effects of the wealth of those that the Liberals see as the hardworking and charitable rich. The concept of the 'individual' is very abstract and it contradicts communalism that sees man only as a member of his concrete community. Neither does it fit to the progressive visions of man as a creative person who is part of his natural and historical global environment. For the Liberals the individualism is the substance of all that is. Such an intellectual background didn't prepare Jinnah to become the leader of the Muslim community in India. For a long time, he considered communal links to be only private links hardly connected to more general issues.

He venerated the Parsee politician and thinker Pherozeshah and Naroji who became the first British MP (Member of Parliament) of Indian origin. They were rather conservative thinkers and his moderation in social and political matters is indebted to their ideas. Jinnah was shortly tempted to become a comedian but his father was so upset that he decided to lead a more conventional life and, back home in 1897, he worked as a lawyer in Bombay main Judicial institution where he was the only Muslim lawyer. He was a modern westernized young man, tall with thin features and an intense look. Unlike Gandhi, who left Western fashions to appear wrapped in a traditional dhoti, Jinnah preferred Western clothes. To the end of his life, he remained faithful to his London tailors, his cigars and good quality whisky. His English was impeccable and some people even said that he mastered it better than Urdu.

At the end of the nineteenth century there were in India some 80,000 public corporal punishments a year, colonial taxes amounted to the double of the pre-colonial taxes, custom duties favoured British goods against Indian industrial goods. Most of the population lived in dire poverty. Twenty million people died in famines in the last quarter of the century. The convicts in the Andaman Islands were around 90 000 prisoners that English doctors used as guinea pigs in their experiments. Workers and farmers were cruelly exploited. India had been in the middle of the eighteenth century the second economic power of the world (after China) but because of colonization and the externalization of its economy in favor of the UK this giant was now shrinking to become a dwarf who represented only 4 % of the world economy when it became independent in 1947.[34] Colonization shouldn't be analyzed as the occupation of another country but as a destructive process of underdevelopment.[35] Although the Western world thought that wars were receding, colonial conquests were going on in Africa and deadly weapons were about to take more lives in the coming century than in the seven preceding centuries.[36]

Jinnah, as a Liberal, could not see the world in such dark lights. He became a member of the INC (Indian National Congress) which he joined in 1904 at the yearly meeting of the Party and, faithful to his taste for Liberal democracy, he followed the political line of moderate leaders like Gokhale. The organization was then a club for the India élite. It had been created after the happenings of 1857 by the British colonial masters in order to have a more accurate feeling of what was happening in their huge colony. In 1857 the British expatriates had been absolutely unprepared to cope with a revolutionary situation because they had been quite unsuspicious of the frustrations and anger of the colonized Indians. As mentioned earlier, the rebellious movement of 1857 started with mutinies in the

---

[34] See Paul Bairoch, 'International Industrialization levels from 1750 to 1980', in *Journal of European Economic History*, N° 11, 2, 1982.
[35] Rosa Luxemburg has brilliantly developed this theme.
[36] Michel Naumann, *MN Roy*, L'Harmattan, Paris, 2006, p 13.

army (the reason why the British chose to call the Sepoy mutiny) but also involved the aristocracy, the Mughal Emperor and millions of people. It completely surprised the East India Company that ruled the colony. The Britishers did not want such a situation to happen ever again so they created the Congress, an Indian party that they could consult to feel the consequences of their rule and alter it if necessary. The Congress was associated to the various political and administrative bodies of the colony but the Party had practically no power.

This situation was becoming more and more problematic as the Indian middle-class was growing in spite of the segregation and the handicaps created by colonization for the dark races. The Indian industrialists could not easily import machines, their production was heavily taxed. Nevertheless, the leaders of the Party remained respectful of the colonial authority but tensions were slowly growing. Already a group of young activists was experimenting mass actions under the guidance of Tilak and members of the petty-bourgeoisie, a class closer to the poor and less infatuated with British ways than the urban bourgeoisie. Jinnah was at ease with the moderate leaders and disliked Tilak. The young lawyer was then in favours of an alliance between the Hindu and the Muslims and he doesn't seem to have objected too much to the fact that Tilak's militant trend was mainly Hindu and used Hinduism (the religion of more than 80 % of the Indians) to create a national feeling: for instance, Tilak and his followers revived and celebrated the Ganesha festivals and their protests were mostly related to claims that defended Hindu traditions and interests. It was obviously easier to create a Hindu nationalist feeling than an Indian one but Jinnah was against these manifestations and the new rising radicalism of some militants within the India National Congress because of their style and not yet because he thought that this new kind of expression ignored the Muslim component of the nation. He was nevertheless the lawyer that Tilak called to his help when he was arrested in 1906 and he did his best to help him. Later he even got an acquittal for Tilak when he was accused of sedition. Jinnah's skills as a lawyer were also established when he fought in the Bombay Caucus Case when the English were trying to favour their own candidates against the Indian politicians who challenged them.

In 1904 he was in contact with the All-India Muslim League whose leaders knew him and sometimes invited him to speak to the members of the organization. In 1913 Jinnah joined the Muslim League while remaining a member of the INC. He also joined, with the ML, the Home Rule League inspired by Annie Besant, an Irish activist who had settled in India. Jinnah was clearly for the unity of both religions, Hinduism and Islam, into a single nation. In 1906 he had harshly criticized a delegation led by the Aga Khan whose purpose was to ask the viceroy to protect the Muslims against the Hindu majority. The Aga Khan latter said that he paved the way that Jinnah was one day to tread. In 1916 Jinnah became the President of the Muslim League and he was instrumental in the Lucknow Pact, an alliance between the All-India Muslim League and the Congress. Two years later he married Maryam Rattanbay Petit, a Parsee. He was obviously a man who seemed beyond regional and religious prejudices. Nevertheless, he did his best to give Muslim laws established rights in the legal system of the colony that tolerated different laws for different communities. [37] Such a tolerance was due to a prejudice that saw European ways as superior to the minds of darker races. Therefore, they should not be forced on inferior people. Another cause of this tolerance was the divide and rule strategy of the colonizers who defended all kinds of community particularism in order divide the colonized.

In 1911 many Muslims were disappointed by the end of the partition of Bengal. This split of Bengal was a project whose purpose was to isolate the Bengali Hindu in two new entities in which they would be overwhelmed by the Biharis, the tribal minorities and the Muslims. The English had always disliked the rich and argumentative Bengali 'babus' and intellectuals whom they saw as hypocrites and malignant people. They preferred those that they called the 'martial races', the Sikhs, the Gurkhas or the Muslims whom they saw as frank, brave and loyal. The Bengali cultural Renaissance of the nineteenth century and the various Nationalist and

---

[37] Stanley Wolpert, *Jinnah of Pakistan*, OUP, New York, 1984, p 33.

Terrorist groups that sprang up in the Eastern part of India at the beginning of the twentieth century had confirmed and even increased the English prejudices against the Bengali. The partition of this province, the richest of India, had met a strong and enduring resistance since 1905. The Bengali militants experimented means of non-violent actions that Gandhi would latter use and finally, after half a decade of tensions, the colonial power reunified Bengal into a single unit where the Hindus still had a scanty majority in spite of the demographic growth the Muslim component. Tagore, the Bengali wise man, then wrote a novel entitled *The House and the World* that foresaw the partition of Bengal and anticipated the disasters of the partition between India and Pakistan. The great writer also stressed in his works the cruelty of nationalist politicians whom he described as men indifferent to the suffering of the people that they cynically manipulate.

The First World War (1914–1918) was a disaster for the colonies of the British Empire. The load was unbearable for India whose contribution to the war was very heavy. Hunger, epidemics, revolts crushed by the army created a post-war situation favourable of course to the terrorist nationalist groups like the Republicans but also to the non-violent line of Gandhi who seemed to rally around him more and more militants and movements. Even Gokhale had paved the way for this disciple of Tolstoy who wanted to take politics and protests at grass-root level. Hindus and Muslims responded to his call. Jinnah spoke against the alliance of the kalifate movement and the INC. The Kalifate, that was at that time defending the pan-Muslim institutions and sacred cities threatened by the defeat of their guardians — Turkey — against the English, was, according to him, an extremist religious group, but the desire for unity was so strong that he could not be understood by the INC that welcomed the Kalifate to strengthen the alliance between the two most numerous religions of India. Jinnah was also opposed to the Gandhi line: The Satyagraha mass protest, in spite of its non-violence, was for Jinnah an open door to anarchy. In fact, Gandhi himself cancelled the movement after months of strikes, boycotts and demonstrations because of growing violence and the burning by protesting crowds of a police building. He was arrested, tried and sent to jail in 1922. This cancelation of a promising and successful mass movement was seen by the Communist M.N. Roy like a betrayal.[38] Nevertheless Gandhi's popularity survived his controversial but moral decision and he retained his hold on the INC and the mass of Indians who had for the first time since 1857 been part of a historical movement that had shattered the colonial power.

Jinnah left the Congress and defended the unity of his Muslim League divided about British propositions of reforms that the INC had promptly rejected. Actually, the British offer was extremely deceptive: the new institutions that they proposed were unlikely to give the colonized any real power whereas the INC expected changes that would lead India towards the status of dominion, that is to say an almost complete independence within the British Commonwealth of nations. Dominions are bound to recognize the Crown and coordinate their foreign policy with England but apart from these constraints they are independent countries. India wanted to enjoy that status already given to Australia, Canada, New Zealand and South Africa but this claim was constantly rebuked. All that the Indian Nationalists were offered was assemblies with electoral colleges that frustrated the universal suffrage and a very limited say in the affairs of the colony.

As a member of the Congress Jinnah had first refused the division of the nation into electoral colleges[39] and favoured a fair expression of the voters through universal suffrage and geographical constituencies, but now, as a Muslim defending his community and the main personality of the ML, he wanted to have an electoral college to give the second religious community of India enough representatives to guarantee the rights of the Muslims. For Ambedkar, the leader of the Dalits (the Untouchables), only the pariahs should be given a special electoral college to correct the many discriminations that paralysed them. Jinnah nevertheless wished one for the Muslims. He remained flexible in his relations on this issue with the INC and often said that he was ready to discuss the terms of an

---

[38] Michel Naumann, op. cit., p 88.
[39] These colleges could concern religions, castes, sexes, Europeans, European traders, Indian traders, landowners, Universities, Anglo-Indians…

agreement on the features and the importance of the Muslim college.

His propositions were known as the 14 points (1928). He claimed decentralization, autonomy and electoral colleges to empower the local Muslim communities, a minimum representation of the Muslims fixed at one third of the local and central assemblies, a specific status for the three major Muslim provinces (Punjab, Bengal and the West frontier province), the split of Sindh and the Bombay presidency, reforms in Baluchistan to regenerate this forgotten part of the colony, fair ratios of Muslim civil servants at all levels, cultural guaranties for the Islamic Faith and regions and total religious freedom all over India. These 14 points aimed at contradicting Nehru's stance in favour of geographical constituencies but Nehru was the rising personality of the Congress and the INC rejected Jinnah's 14 points.

This failure led him to withdraw from public responsibilities. In 1930, he left the ML and India and sailed to England, soon followed by his sister Fatima who joined him in the United Kingdom. The Muslim community had lost her most brilliant negotiator and the ML a very competent leader so in 1933 the Muslim League and Iqbal asked him to come back home and resume his commitments to the League and the defence of Islam in India. The Muslim separatist issue had progressed among intellectuals and members of the élite but the ML was still unable to capture a strong Muslim vote so the militants hoped that Jinnah's return would improve the situation of the Party. He was back in India and at the head of the ML in 1934. By then the word Pakistan had been invented by Choudhary Rahmat Ali in a pamphlet that claimed the creation of a Muslim entity around the Indus Valley.[40] This bold project was to become more and more appealing to the ML and Jinnah but it required more time to become a concrete hope for the majority of the Muslim population.

Endless negotiations between the Indians and the English, interrupted by militant actions, finally produced in 1935 a project that the INC found acceptable. London had finally conceded a more

---

[40] Iftikar Malik, *History of Pakistan*, Greenwood Press, Wesport, 2008, p 121.

democratic vote in the eight provinces of the colony whereas the centre remained dominated by the colonial administration. In 1937 the INC won a crushing electoral victory in all the provinces. The Congress, obviously elated by this success refused to form any government with the Muslim League. Had the INC been more conscious of the possibility of a partition of India, the winners of the elections would have shared the victory with the Muslim League to prove that a common future was safe for the minority. Unfortunately, the success of the Congress was such that the request of the ML was not seriously studied. Jinnah was traumatized by this attitude and the exclusion of his Party which he saw as the proof that the Muslims would become a marginalized community after independence.[41] Even the North-West that would one day become Pakistan was conquered by the INC. The good results of the ML in Delhi were obvious but even there the League could not emerge as a ruling force and was excluded from the local government. Suddenly the frightening vision of a coming Hindu State struck Jinnah.

For the Congress the ML was excluded but not the Muslims because many of them were militants of the INC who would share as Indians the available provincial positions with the Hindu militants. This position was understandable because the elections had given the INC a clear majority and for them Indians at large, Hindus and Muslims, had given them their votes. They thought they had overcome the Hindu / Muslim problem. It is also likely that if the INC endlessly repeated that it was the Party of all the Indians, a number of militants and leaders, consciously for some and unconsciously for the others, couldn't see the difference between Hindu nationalism and Indian nationalism and they thought that the problems between the two religious communities could be solved by hushing the voice of the Muslims expressed by the ML. Another argument can also explain the attitude of the Congress leaders: many members of the Muslim community had still retained the Aga Khan habit to beg for English protection, which made them untrusted allies likely to turn anytime towards the enemy. Actually, one could say that the INC by dropping suddenly the ML was

---

[41]   Jawant Singh, *Jinnah*, OUP, Oxford, 2009, p 188.

pushing the Muslims towards Pakistan and towards the English. Almost no one within the INC guessed that the exclusion of the ML from all positions of power in the provinces was a mistake whose consequences would soon appear.

The mood in the League was going from frustration to bitterness and even a desire of revenge. It came a few years later, with World War II, when the English refused to concede Indian independence to gain Indian loyalty in the war against Germany. The Congress then had to make a clear choice: struggle for independence or remain in power in the provinces and work with people who refused to commit themselves to any tangible promises and remained so vague about the post-war period. In the First World War the Indians made the mistake to believe that their loyalty would be rewarded with deep reforms but the English offers after the war had been ridiculous. The Congress was not ready to make twice the same mistake. In 1942 the INC abandoned all the positions conquered in 1937 in order to launch a decisive 'Quit India' defiance campaign. The ML leaders saw this decision as a historical chance to get rid of what they saw as a Hindu rule and they accepted to remain faithful to the colonial masters at war against Germany and Japan. The National movement was therefore split according to political strategies linked somehow to different religions. Jinnah's decision was of course understandable but it was nevertheless a mistake because the divorce between the nationalist cause and the ML prevented the Muslim community to be part of the struggle for independence and put them in the situation of getting Pakistan from the English instead of forging a nation in the struggle for the Independence of Pakistan.

Jinnah then had to build a stronger ML beyond the elitist group of intellectuals who had started to believe in the claim of separation and Pakistan. It was not an easy task. Most Muslims were poor farmers whose economic and social problems were not a ML priority because leaders and militants belonged to wealthy classes. Muslim electors preferred to vote for local politicians who were landlords who ruled their constituencies like prey birds and knew how to speak to the local poor. To the Muslim farmers exploited by feudal landlords the national and international issues as presented by the ML were pointless. The best politicians of the Muslim community were often Gandhi's friends like Azad who chaired the INC, Ghafar Khan who developed non-violence in the territories of what is now North Pakistan, Ajmal Khan the specialist of education or Zakir Hussein who would become President of India. In Bengal, Fazlul Huq, the lawyer of the poor farmers, had created a Party that had conquered the poor Muslims' vote but he had to vie with Chandra Bhose, often called Netaji, the popular rival of Gandhi within the INC, whose populist discourse and militant actions had given him the vote of the poor Hindu farmers and workers. In Bengal the Muslims were now the majority. Surawardhi, who controlled the Muslim conservative vote, was manipulating the ML while he was not excluding the independence of Bengal from his half secret wishes about the future of his region. In Punjab, the feudal lord Sir Sikander seemed only interested in local issues and, as a typical prey-bird politician he didn't like to fly out of his territory. Actually, he had no taste for national issues unless they threatened or favoured his class. For the *ulama* Pakistan or Delhi politics were vague realities and they knew that the Muslim minorities in the Hindu regions were more numerous than the majority Muslims of the North-West of India and Bengal, which made Pakistan a not very appealing claim for them.

Jinnah, backed by his faithful and talented friend Liaquat Ali Khan, nevertheless conquered the Muslim vote and militancy. First the ML positions recently acquired when the INC abandoned the governments of the eight provinces and when the ML rallied the colonial government gave his party an experience of the corridors of power. He skilfully used his warm relations with the English to bring about the cause of Pakistan and he dominated his Muslim rivals to make the ML the party of most Muslims and of one single claim: Pakistan, the land of the pure. The death of Sir Sikander gave him Punjab because the great local leader left behind him too many competing candidates for his succession. In Bengal Surawardhi finally decided to work with the ML. Last but not least: the British often saw the issue of Pakistan as an opportunity to use their old divide and rule strategy and they hoped to retain a prevailing position in South Asia as the referees between two rival States, India and Pakistan, both also controlled through the Commonwealth as dominions. The complexity of the situation put Jinnah's Pakistan on a rather conservative road: it is quite obvious that Pakistan had become a realistic option but not at all a revolutionary one and anyway the project depended so much from the English that the struggle for independence now hardly concerned the ML. If Jinnah dreamed of an Islamic Republic that would offer the minorities all the rights provided by a Liberal State, the unity of the Muslims involved rallying powerful conservative groups by not giving too much consideration to the poor Muslim farmers and workers.

The 'Quit India' defiance mass campaign was hard and bitter but it was a success. At the end of the Second World War, no one could deny that the Independence of the colonial territory was in view. The Indian crowds knew it and the colonial masters felt it was the end of almost two centuries of presence and domination in India. Obviously, no one could go against the trend set by Gandhi but the question of Pakistan had to be settled anyway. When the British wanted to have an idea of the ML projects for India after the war, Jinnah had launched a committee whose work produced the ML Lahore resolution in favour of Pakistan.[42] When the British negotiator, Cripps, offered to all the components of India a 'local option' instead of just a partition between India and Pakistan, Jinnah remained unsatisfied because he still feared that the ML was not yet in command of Muslim opinion everywhere. With most ML leaders, he favoured a pre-independence decision made at the top. He wanted the English to commit themselves because he disliked the idea of a duel between the Muslims and the Hindus. Jinnah made clear, during his talks with Gandhi in 1944, that the issue of Pakistan had to be settled before the departure of the colonial masters of India, that is to say in trilateral discussions.

The Simla negotiations with the Viceroy, Wavell, about the transition towards independence, were tense because Nehru and Jinnah' many clashes, but it was interrupted by the English elections that saw the surprising victory of Atlee's Labour Party in 1945. Churchill, a difficult partner for India that he disliked and even

---

[42] Ayesha Jalal, *The Sole Spokesman*, CUP, Cambridge, 1994, pp 54–58.

hated, was defeated. Everybody in India hoped that the Labour Party would be more flexible than the old lion who thought that without the pearl of the Empire England would not be a world power anymore. The elections for an Indian Constitutional Assembly were won by the INC but the ML got this time 75 % of the Muslim vote. It was the proof that Jinnah's line on Pakistan had won the hearts of many Muslims. If any doubt, in 1946, the National Protest Day organized by the ML showed, unfortunately after riots and bloody communal fighting, that the separatist issue could not be ignored. Atlee wanted to go fast and he sent Mountbatten as the new Viceroy to settle everything before 1948. An interim Government was set with Nehru at its head. Jinnah wanted parity between Muslims and Hindus in the number of ministries given but he finally dropped this claim against a veto about all issues connected with the Muslim community. Relations between Jinnah and Nehru were very tense: whenever Jinnah called the two decolonized states to be carved out of colonial India Pakistan and Hindustan, the second term always upset Nehru who was angry because for him the Indian Republic to come would be a secular State open to all the Indians and not a religious State for the Hindus.

The INC and especially Nehru's socialists wanted a strong central State that could launch socialist economic plans so they finally accepted the idea of partition as a better deal than all the projects of decentralisation invented by the English to reassure the Muslims and create a loose unit rather difficult to rule from the centre in Delhi.[43] A weak and hardly manageable India was probably the secret hope of the colonial lobby that hoped that the new independent State would need so much the help of the former colonizer that imperial rule would survive independence. Jinnah insisted that the army and India's public assets should be divided. The Radcliffe commission for a border between India and Pakistan did a most incompetent work on inaccurate maps and the results of a very old Census. Mountbatten kept the border secret before the independences of India and Pakistan by the middle of august 1947.

---

[43] Yasmin Khan, *The Great Partition,* Yale University Press, New Haven, 2008, pp 85–86.

Jinnah had to be everywhere during the process that gave birth to Pakistan. Already the various regions of Pakistan had to be coordinated by his authority that prevented local rulers to forget that they were part of a whole. He was the soul and backbone of the new country. Partition was a human disaster: families who, because of their religion, were found on the wrong side of the border were aggressed, 14 million and a half-displaced people suffered violence and loss of property, massacres happened on both sides of the border. The human casualties have been officially evaluated at one million but most specialists think that this amount should be doubled. Kashmir, a state with a Muslim majority and a Hindu dynasty, was soon the cause of the first war between India and Pakistan. The new nation survived anyway in spite of these tragedies but Jinnah was exhausted. His lungs were everyday weaker and he often needed long periods of time to rest. He only had one more year to live.

Jinnah is the one without whom Pakistan might not have become a reality. His political life went through several stages:

- The years of formation, which includes his exposure to the liberal ideas that made him a moderate politician and a man who was not easily attracted by communalism and not easily tempted to connect politics and religion.
- As an INC member nostalgic of moderate leaders like Gokhale, he could not accept the new militant and mass movement that prevailed within the INC from 1920. Simultaneously he fought against the Kalifate and took the leadership of the more political and liberal Muslim League.
- After a self-inflicted political exile, he came back to India and linked more and more his career to the Pakistan project that became the one claim of the Muslim League. If he was very rigid on the issue of a separate Muslim state, he never forgot his liberal ideals and he saw Pakistan as a very open and tolerant Islamic Republic.

Still nowadays, when people are victimized in Pakistan, they remind their rulers of Jinnah's commitments to democracy and human rights. Jinnah's paradox is that to create an Islamic nation he invoked values and rights that the mass of his followers did not really know and understand because colonization had not pulled them out of a traditional world vision. He imagined a people for Pakistan and mistook the anxieties of the Muslims confronting the Hindu majority for a national feeling. Pakistan was, in spite of the hopes of some, a negative entity, the result of fear, not really what a nation should be: the struggle against the risk of a Hindu domination unified the people but once the fear removed the divisions in the country and within the Muslims reappeared.

It was so because Jinnah's innate moderation, liberal sympathies and skilful courting of the English took him and his closest friends far from the kind of great anti-colonial struggle that forged the nation in Egypt, Algeria or Cuba. He wanted a nation guaranteed by England but England could only give him a State because the national feeling could only come from the effort to break the colonial and feudal chains. For some time, Jinnah's prestige could hide the flaws of the national consciousness of the new State. When he died, Pakistan had to live without the father and founder of the country and without a strong national consciousness. It is still a protonation whose creative project is yet to come to life because it is in limbo, undefined, unclear to the people and hovering like a ghost over scattered regions, cultures, religions, various conceptions of time and history, local and world conflicts, contradictory influences, ruling classes that cannot really fulfil their national mission, real economy and parallel economy…

Independence with just hard bargaining with the colonizers (mainly on borders and guarantees for the Moslems against a so-called Hindi Raj) and without a real anticolonial struggle has a cost. It creates a gap between traditional cultures and the modern culture supposed to come with the Nation-State. The struggle for Pakistan looked more like a communal claim than a fight against the British Empire. Conservative regressions remain a risk when these two cultures, the old traditional one and the new national and decolonized one, are not properly unified. This contradiction can only be overcome in the process of a liberation struggle that uses and adapts traditional significations to the progressive needs of the liberation of the subdued people while creating a solidarity that connects the scattered traditional components of the protonation to a common progressive goal. This process of transmutation of old values into new functional values could not really take place in Pakistan.

It still remains to be done.

CHAPTER III: THE HISTORY OF PAKISTAN

The birth of Pakistan on the 15th of August 1947 raised the hopes of the many but hid the anxiety of those who were conscious that the colonial policy and the drawing of the borders of the two new states had given the Muslims a rural and feudal country deprived of industries and modern administration. A thin westernized élite and a few civil servants were in charge of two units (Western Pakistan and Eastern Pakistan) separated by India. Each part of Pakistan was a mosaic of peoples, religions and languages. The pillars of the unity of the young State were Islam and the rejection of India, one positive, the other negative, but it was not illegitimate to suspect that the first pillar would not really be strong without the second one. Both forces were hiding destructive trends: the rejection of India was a threat for the future of all the new nations of the subcontinent and the modern forms of Islam that prevailed in the dreams of the founders — politicians as well as thinkers — obviously lacked the flexibility of Akbar or of the old traditions that accommodated diversity into a rich and tolerant way of life in the past.
The politicians of the Muslim League took over in 1947 as the founders of this new entity. This section of the élite failed to create a viable State and the other sections which took advantage of this failure were not able to do better.

- The lack of audacity of the Nation's Fathers in sketching a constitution that would combine unity and diversity produced quarrels and divisions.
- Ten years after Independence these politicians stepped back to let the army and the bureaucrats impose their competences which they saw as neutral and modern instead of the biased and quarrelling attitudes of the politicians, but the offices and the barracks were too rigid and they turned their back to Democracy. A group of these soldiers, to unite and discipline the people, even introduced conservative religious forces into the corridors of power.

Waves of demonstrations of angry civilians and distressed people wanted the return of Democratic rule and a social policy to overcome the discrepancies between classes and regions, and the politicians were back in office to lead the country (1988–1999).

Nevertheless, during this period and after, they could never ignore the deep State established by the Security services and the generals and when the Afghan wars as well as the nuclear issues of the subcontinent brought Pakistan to become a very important actor of world politics, the situation became even more complicated: in the last decade of the twentieth century and the first two decades of the twenty-first century, civil wars, unrest coming from conservative religious forces, corrupt democracy and coups combined to delay the economic development and the social measures that would have saved Pakistan from division and instability.

The Politicians and Founding Fathers

The Muslim and Hindu populations of the former colony (India) had to suffer communal riots and a dramatic exodus to Pakistan or to the Indian Republic to be protected by the borders of their new country. No one should nevertheless forget that this protective function was hypocritical in so far as the creation of States with a religious identity was the consequence of the project of the politicians who linked Independence and nationality to religion: those who caused the disturbances were those who offered shelters! The legitimacy of the State was rather weird. Partition was a heavy price to be paid by commoners and victimized communities. India had not been partitioned but torn.

In 1947 these dramatic events were still in everybody's mind and the new born entity called Pakistan stood simultaneously shattered by what had recently happened and hopeful about what was to come. Unfortunately, the curse of religious nationalism was not behind the politicians in charge. The monster was still alive and Hindus, Sikhs and Christians were unsafe in Pakistan in spite of Jinnah's and Liaqat Ali Khan's desire to respect their rights. The religious problems and the rivalry with India converged when, against the advice of Liaqat Ali Khan, the Prime Minister who disagreed on the issue with Jinnah, Patan forces from Pakistan attacked the Himalayan State of Kashmir where the ruling Dogra Hindu Dynasty, with the blessing of Indian hard liners, had prevailed over a Muslim population to make this kingdom a part of India. The Pashtun (or Patan) culture has been defined as aristocratic and warlike[44] and Nehru understood the threat immediately. The Indian army intervened and in 1949 the United Nations ceasefire restored peace and ended the first Indo-Pakistani war. Two thirds of Kashmir remained Indian, one third Pakistani. Nehru, the Indian Prime Minister rejected the UN proposition of a referendum as Pakistan still occupied a part of the disputed territory.

This unsolved problem was to cause wars and tensions between the two countries. The Kashmir problem also contributed to associate national politics with Western Pakistan, the component more involved in this confrontation, and made Bengal appear as a less important component of the Union. Baluchistan, in the west of Western Pakistan, was also in turmoil.

Pakistan suffered a loss in the last days of 1948 when the nation lost her main founder and her Governor, Jinnah. He had for too long refused to treat a tenacious tuberculosis because he was afraid that political opponents would take advantage of his health and he did not want to reveal this weakness to those who trusted him so much. The country was struck by another death two years later. Liaquat Ali Khan, who had been a close collaborator of Jinnah and the Prime Minister from the beginning of the creation of Pakistan, was the obvious successor of Jinnah at the head of the new Nation, but had to face the difficult questions (both linguistic and territorial) raised by the coming constitution and he was assassinated in 1951. Liaqat Ali Khan could have been murdered by a Pashtun who wanted his ethnic group to join Afghanistan but as the murderer was lynched by the crowd of witnesses who saw him shoot the Prime Minister and as the documents of the enquiry were lost in a plane crash, the issue has remained blurred. As a Pakistani from

---

[44] Laurent Dessart, *Les Pashtounes, économie et culture d'une aristocratie guerrière*, Harmattan, Paris, 2001.

Punjab and Awd, he could have been the victim of a plot launched by politicians born in what was to become Pakistan. His death did reinforce the sons of the soil (against the Muhadjirs, mostly Sindhi Muslims who had arrived in Pakistan as victims of Partition) and the Punjabis saw themselves as the heart of the new nation. Traditionalists could also have disliked Liaqat Ali Khan's tendency to modernize Islam when he linked Islam and Democracy. Socialists did not like his economic plan based on helps to the private sector and illusions about the trickling down effect. The United States, already eager to make Pakistan a close ally against Communism, might have disliked Liaquat's reluctance to back them in the Korean civil war.

A Bengali, Nazimundin, formerly the Governor of Pakistan, replaced him as Prime Minister (1951–1953) and after him Ali Bogra became Prime Minister (1953–1955). The politicians were often landlords educated at Aligarh, the famous school and University created by Sayyid Ahmad Khan and whose spirit was inspired by the British Public Schools and a very aristocratic ethos. They had a political experience acquired in the Muslim League and the struggle against the Indian Congress. Most were conservative and conscious of their links with the English officials and politicians who favoured Partition, they felt that they needed an Anglo-Saxon godfather and they saw their alliance with the USA, the Western superpower, as a continuation of this protection. Unlike many Third World leaders they had no sympathy for Russia and Socialist ideas. The debates on the Constitution in the fifties had unfortunate results for the future as Eastern Pakistan (Bengal) became a minor component of the Union and Western Pakistan prevailed. In 1954 the elections were a confrontation between the Muslim League and a motley coalition of opponents. Obviously, the leading politicians were under suspicion and not only from Eastern eyes (Bengal) but even from Western eyes. Chaudi Muhamad Ali (Muslim League) then became the new Prime Minister.

In 1956 the Constitution that made Pakistan the first self-proclaimed Islamic State was adopted in spite of its biased features in favour of Western Pakistan. Urdu for instance prevailed over Bengali and the centralization of Pakistan from Karachi and Islamabad was detrimental to Dacca in the East. Iskander Mizra, formerly the Governor General, became the President. To reassure the Bengali, Hussein Shahid Surhrawardi, from the Awami League that defended Eastern interests, was appointed Prime Minister. In Eastern Pakistan progressive politicians and militants disliked Surhrawardi's primitive anti-communism and his acceptance of a US commission that was to supervise the National Army choked many citizens. The repartition of funds between the two parts of Pakistan was always a hot issue and Suhrawardi could not really go against the trend which favoured the centre (situated in Karachi and Islamabad) against the far away east. Iskander Mizra forced him to resign in 1957.

The tensions between East and West then became very acute and Mizra, who was a former soldier, was not patient with the politicians who were entangled in a constitution which could not rule fairly two countries separated by thousands of kilometres. In addition to this contradiction, social inequality in rural and urban zones and the difficulties suffered by the forgotten peripheries of the west (Baluchistan in the South and the Pashtun zone in the north) were shocking. Pakistan really looked as a country which could not be governed and the Constitution could not work miracles. The President therefore, after appointing four Prime Ministers in two years of rule (1956–1958), looked for help among the soldiers. With their very British notion of public service beyond political interests they thought that they could hold the Nation together. This alliance between the President and the army was to put an end to the rule of the politicians and bring about the rule of the bureaucratic élite of the centre whose spearhead was the army.[45]

The Generals and the Bureaucrats

Martial law was first entrusted to General Ayub Khan by the President. He became Prime Minister and abolished the 1956 Constitution. The 1958 coup was justified by the passivity of Iskander Mizra

---

[45] Margaret Smith clearly argued about the opposition between soldiers and politicians in her book on African politics, *A barrel of a Gun*. We have used her sociological conclusion to analyse coups and returns to democracy in Pakistan.

in the issue raised by water management projects in India that threatened Pakistani agriculture. The Prime Minister, as a soldier, felt bound to defend national interests threatened by Indian claims but it was also obvious that the soldiers had stepped into politics to stay for a long time. The 1965 presidential elections were nevertheless an occasion for the civilians to come back. Fatima Jinnah, the sister of the father of the nation stood against Ayub Khan. Born in 1893, she studied at the University of Calcutta and opened a dental surgery clinic in Bombay in 1923. She became an active member of the Muslim League and created a Women's Relief Committee during the partition. This commitment gave birth to the All-Pakistan's Women Association whose purpose was to improve women's lot in the new nation. By then she had become the Mother of the Nation (Mader-e-Millat) and as such she was a formidable opponent for Ayub Khan, but the military power was well entrenched and the frauds during the vote gave the general the mandate he wanted. Fatima Jinnah died in 1967 in Karachi from a heart attack.

The military regime started an agricultural reform that distributed one fifth of the land and it released in 1962 a new constitution based on the substitution of 80,000 selected citizens to the universal suffrage. In 1965 Ayub Khan led the Gibraltar operation to infiltrate the part of Kashmir occupied by the Indian army and helped the Kashmiri guerrillas, which led to a second war between India and Pakistan. In 1966, one year after a rather disastrous war against India, Ayub Khan signed an agreement with the Indian Prime Minister that shocked the patriotic feelings of many citizens. He also tried to curb the conservative Muslim trends.

The Indo-Pakistani war had provoked a massive withdrawal of investments. Austerity came as a direct consequence and the rigid military rule became more and more unpopular. Corruption was growing and most efforts to reduce inequality were dropped. It appeared that Pakistan was still the country of 22 extremely rich families. Fatima Jinnah took the lead of the protest movement and tried to revive the Muslim League in Punjab and in Western Pakistan. In Sindh the PPP (Progressive Party of Pakistan), although it was the creation of a rich landlord, Ali Buttho, was more and more appealing as it tried to break from the very conservative tone of the political class. In Bengal the Awami League proposed socialism and equality for the East whose economy was plundered by the West that channelled State funds to its advantage. The students were voicing the progressive third-world targets of many other new nations: self-reliance, social progress, commitment to anti-colonial and anti-imperialist causes. Nasser, Castro, Mao, Ho Chi Minh, Ben Bella, Nkrumah, Lumumba, Neto were read and admired by the new generations of most third-world countries. Demonstrations in Karachi and Dacca protested against the rigidity of the military caste and Ayub Khan was forced to withdraw in 1969.

He was replaced by another Pashtun general, Yayia Khan, who promised a quick return to Democracy. But the elections were a success for the PPP in the West, and the Awami League of Mujibur Rahman in the East. Although the Awami League had more MPs, Buttho was called by Yayia Khan to form the new government. Protests resumed in Bengal and Yayia Khan's repressive action was incredibly brutal: 10 million people were exiled, between 200,000 and 400,000 women were raped, 1 million Eastern citizens were killed. Biharis, Urdu speakers (Bengali was the language of the majority in the East) who were in favour of Western Pakistan, were massacred by nationalist militants in favour of Bangladesh. The number of victims remains unknown but specialists think that it could be evaluated to several hundreds of thousands. Maoist militants, running away from the cities, started rural guerrillas against the Pakistani army but the revolutionary process was interrupted by an Indian blitzkrieg that freed Eastern Pakistan and led to the independence of Bangladesh. (1971) For India the bold decision to back Bangladesh was due to a couple of political considerations: (1) to weaken Pakistan who had from the start been a very difficult neighbour, and (2) to prevent a Maoist rise that could have overcome India as well as Pakistan.

Buttho became the Prime Minister of Pakistan, now reduced to its Western part. His impact on the political life of his country was to remain prestigious as much as complex and paradoxical.[46] In the name of Islamic Socialism, he nationalized several industrial

---

[46] Denis Hocquet, *Zulficar Ali, le Premier des Buttho*, Harmattan, Paris, 2009.

sectors and the banks but his agrarian reform hardly provided land for 1 % of the rural poor. He created the ISI (Inter-Services Intelligence) that was to become very powerful. Ali Buttho also initiated the process to give Pakistan the status of nuclear power because he thought that this weapon would prevent military disasters such as the one which happened in 1971. He courted Muslim authorities by conceding to the conservative Jamaat-e-Islami that Ahmadis were not Muslims. In 1977 he was re-elected with an almost unbelievable majority that exposed his manipulation of the elections and before he could organize more honest elections he was ousted by the coup of General Zia-ul-Haq and sentenced to death for the murder in an ambush of the father of one of his rivals within the PPP many years ago. The trial was anything but fair. His execution gave his party and his family the aura of martyrdom which is one of the reasons for their future electoral victories after the long and bloody reign of General Zia.

He was a Punjabi and a British officer who had decided to live in Pakistan. As a soldier he fought against the Indian army in 1965 and as an expert sent to Jordan where he crushed the progressive Palestinian revolt of September 1970 against King Hussein. In spite of that he was appointed Head of Staff by Ali Buttho and he betrayed him by launching the second coup of the history of Pakistan. Harsh and conservative, this pro-American ruler was to stay at the head of the State for a decade.

The new ruler was strengthened by the conservative religious parties that he courted when he made the Sha'aria the source of the judicial power in Pakistan and contemplated the creation of a Caliphate. The Jamaat-i-Islami was the most important Islamic Party. Created in 1941, it was originally against Pakistan as the partition was bound to split the Ummah (the community of the believers) and against the Muslim League, but once the new State was established the Party decided to make sure that the new nation was faithful to its Islamic commitments. The Jamaat-i-Islami was of course not ready to give a progressive interpretation of Islam like Buttho or even a modernist one like Liaquat Ali Khan. This conservative stance survived to the dictator and is still the cause of cruel punishments and constant harassment of the believers of all creeds. The

Constitution Zia wanted for his country was also carved for him and his personal power. He won a referendum that linked the issue of Islamic Law and his own power in 1984 and organized elections in 1985 without the MRD (Movement to Restore Democracy). He made Junejo his faithful Prime Minister. With the help of China whose relations with India were tense because of their rivalry for the domination of the Himalaya, Pakistan got her "Islamic Atomic Bomb", which created in the region the possibility of a nuclear war between India and Pakistan. Zia remained a close friend of the United States and improved his country's warm relations with China, India's great rival in Asia.

The Afghan resistance to the Soviet invasion made Pakistan the local manager of the US and Saudi aid to the Mujahidins. Selling arms and drugs did not help reduce corruption and ISI became a state within the state as the organization which backed the CIA in the struggle against the Russians in Afghanistan. Zia and ISI decided to help Hekmatyar, the most conservative war chief of the Afghan guerrilla, and always opposed Masood who was more open to democratic values. ISI also intervened to oppose the guerrillas who were for the independence of Kashmir instead of joining Pakistan. The powerful security and information institution (ISI) created the Hizbul Mujahidins to that effect and launched the Laskar-e-Taiba which was to become the first terrorist movement in South Asia.

As drugs from Afghanistan were most important in funding the resistance to the Soviet invasion, Pakistan, as a close neighbour, became more involved in illegal traffics and Pakistanis became the first victims of these products. The number of consumers of drugs arounds 6 % of the whole population, which is a very high ration. Opium travels from north-west to south, towards the coast of the sea of Oman, Karachi and the border with Iran. Local farmers are involved in their production all along the border with Afghanistan where illegal laboratories work for powerful cartels that tend to create connections with the administration.

The influence of the two donators of funds and weapons for the Jihadists, the USA and Saudi Arabia, increased their hold on Pakistan. Actually, very early, Saudi Arabia had started courting

Pakistan. In 1971 Jeda backed their ally against Bangladesh and India. Zia was seen as a man who could back Islamic countries and Muslims in general. During the Afghan wars the Saudis also started financing Madrasas. They are sometimes called upon to arbitrate local conflicts in Pakistan. As the Saudi army, well provided in modern weapons but not always very efficient during wars, does not look too reliable, many people think that the Pakistani army could defend the Saudi regime and the royal family in case of an emergency. Many Pakistanis work in the Gulf (often in very severe conditions which involve a complete lack of rights) and send money back home through the networks of the hawaladars who appeared for some of them as early as the Middle Ages. The work of these migrants and the funds they provide Pakistan with are also good reasons to make the Saudi-Pakistani connection worthwhile and long lasting.

In 1988 Zia died in a plane crash. The President of the Senate, Ghulam Ishak Khan, took over according the rules of the Constitution and he organized open elections that the PPP was to win. The new leader of the Party was Benazir Buttho, the daughter of Ali Buttho. She had made sure that she and the PPP were always seen as the most important opponent to the dictator.

The politicians were back for a decade.

A Decade of Alternation

The return to democracy could not eradicate the deep State carved for themselves by ISI, mafias and Islamic extremists and the shadow of the still powerful generals hanged over the alternation of two parties both ruled by rich landowners and each based on one region: Sindh for the PPP and Punjab for the Muslim League of Pakistan led by Nawaz Sharif.

From 1988 to 1990 Benazir Buttho was Prime Minister. It was a transition period, both for her country and the region where the withdrawal of the Russian forces in Afghanistan opened a paradoxical period of uncertainty due to the fight between rivals in Afghanistan. Since Thatcher and Reagan, the trend was to privatize the economic units created in the preceding period during which the economic system was capitalistic but the pilot was the State. The US Godfather of Pakistan expected her to comply to the new liberal creed and she had to do so. She also had a lot to learn about how to rule a country like Pakistan. She did not privatize the economy as much as she promised and therefore indirectly wrote the platform of her opponent for the next legislation: he just had to swear that he would go further than her in the process of privatization. She also led a difficult battle against Ghulam Ishak Khan for appointments in the civil service and the army and he dismissed her. She lost the coming elections but nevertheless retained her hold on Sindh, her stronghold.

Nawaz Sharif, leader of the Muslim League of Pakistan (MLP), from Punjab, became Prime Minister and his liberal economic governance was most welcome by the rich and the North American Godfather of Pakistan. The country needed a plan for the peripheric regions which could not come with a dispensation based on the withdrawal of the State. It had hardly come with Benazir Buttho, but most people still felt that she could give more than her rival and in 1993 she won the elections.

Her rule from 1993 to 1996 was more convincing than between 1988 and 1990. She had learned how to cope with such a diverse and difficult political environment but she made a tragic mistake: she yielded to the very conservative Jamiat-Ulema-e- Islami (that provided the ideological formation of youngsters who became the Talibans) and also to the powerful ISI: she let the Talibans loose on Afghanistan. Taught in conservative religious institutions, backed by conservative Islamic parties, trained by ISI, they were mostly Pashtuns from both sides of the Afghan border called the Durand line, a colonial border never recognized by an international institution. In Afghanistan they were the most numerous ethnic groups. Traditionally and according to institutions such as the tribal assembly, they provided kings and ruled this motley country. The ethnic groups of the North, Tajiks and Turkmen, did not accept this invasion and resisted under the guidance of war leaders such as Masood. For ISI and the army, Afghanistan as a friendly neighbour under their control would provide a rear space in case of an Indian attack on Pakistan. For the politicians and the economic actors, pushing northward to get an access to the oil and gas of Central Asia was a security for the future. The "Great Game" of Kipling and the English colonizers to contain the Russians in Central Asia was ascribed in the late twentieth century and the early twenty-first century to new superpowers such as China (to replace Russia) and the USA (to replace the UK) and sub-imperialists such as India, Pakistan, Turkey, Russia and Iran.

Benazir Buttho lost her position on a charge of clan violence, corruption and nepotism and escaped to Dubai. Nawaz Sharif was back as Prime Minister but his poor handling of the Kargil war in Kashmir against India angered the Generals and put an end to the democratic experience of alternance between the PPP and the MLP when General Musharraf took over in 1999. The new ruler was a Pakistani born in colonial India in a family who settled in Pakistan after partition. Part of his education took place in Turkey, a country he loved. He had joined the army in 1964 and Nawaz Sharif appointed him as head of Staff.

This new coup brought Pakistan into the twenty-first century.

Pakistan in the Twenty-First Century

Musharraf very quickly re-established civilian rule but he went into politics, created his own party and became President. He negotiated with Benazir Buttho her comeback to Pakistani politics but she was murdered by a suicide bomber in 2008, just before the elections. ISI, the Taliban and Musharraf himself were suspected but her tragic death has remained a mystery. The PPP won the polls and ruled for a few years.

Musharraf had to follow the USA in their war against the Taliban and Al-Qaeda in Afghanistan after 11/9/2001. ISI had, simultaneously, to back the North-Americans and protect the Taliban whose alliance with the Pashtun clans of the mountains of Pakistan was enduring. The Pakistani army had to go through a cruel civil war against them. Islamabad had to tolerate North-American strikes and bombing against the Taliban and their allies in Pakistan.

The relations of Pakistan with the Moslem world are as complex as Pakistan's relations with the West or India. For years Saudi Arabia helped financially this Islamic Republic who offered Ryad a strong army (equipped by the USA) that would protect the rich princes of the cradle of Islam against Nasser. Pakistani migrant workers and business people came to the Gulf and remitted their salaries and gains to their country. These financial relations favoured the BCCI of Agha Hassan Abedi, from Karachi, but this alluring and successful Islamic Bank went too far in infiltrating the US financial system and it was denounced as a rogue Bank linked to drug money, arms and dictators. Libya too was close to Pakistan during the period that gave birth to the Islamic bomb. Later, during the Arab spring of 2011 Pakistani men went to Bharein to help the conservative forces to check the democratic protest. Many Pakistani people idealized the relations between their country and the cradle of Islam but actually the link with the Arab kings is not as strong as it seems. First, it is obvious that Pakistan would not openly challenge the Shi'ite State of Iran because Islamabad doesn't want a civil war between Sunnites and Shi'ites at home, which means that Saudi Arabia cannot trust Pakistan too much against Teheran. Second, the USA needs Pakistan to check the regional Islamist movements inspired by the wahabites from Arabia. The "link" with the parts of the world from where Islam comes is also a knot of contradictions.

Many acts of terrorism and religious unrest also struck urban zones of Punjab and other regions. The situation in South Asia, from the Himalayas to Sri Lanka, was then very tense. In 2008, the President, Asif Ali Zardari, pressurized by Washington, the anti-Taliban Kaboul Government and India, had to dismantle the terrorist movement Lashkar-e-Taiba (called "T").[47] The group, backed by ISI, wanted to create an Islamic state in India and transform Pakistan into a "real" Islamic state. The "T" had attacked the Indian Parliament in 2001, creating a threat of nuclear confrontation between Delhi and Islamabad, and in 2007 a terrorist attack was launched in Bombay. The "T" also blew up the US embassy of Kabul. Its men

---

[47] Jean Luc Racine, 'Au Pakistan un Président sous influence', in *Le Monde Diplomatique*, Aout 2008, p 17.

were very active in Kashmir, especially against the Kashmiri movement that worked for a country independent from Delhi and Islamabad. Like ISI they backed the Taliban and offered them sanctuaries in Pakistan. For some time already the CIA had stopped working with ISI — a very treacherous and difficult partner indeed — and wanted the powerful intelligence service of Pakistan to drop the "T", the Taliban and their allies in the Pashtun parts of Pakistan.[48]

The US pressures to dismantle the "T" aimed to get rid of this dangerous terrorist group but also to separate the politicians from ISI and the army. They hoped that they could make Pakistan a more coherent and decent ally. Obama seemed to have thought that the region could become more peaceful with free politicians who were more likely to develop new links with India than politicians under the military wings.[49] The military wanted to keep control of the foreign policy with India whose policy involved holding Kashmir and her heights because the one who owns the roof owns the house. The Indians were also trying to get an access to the energy resources of Central Asia and they courted Afghanistan. The Pakistani generals, who felt responsible for the nation's security and future in the region, had therefore to keep a hold on the civilian rulers' policy about India, Kashmir and Afghanistan and since Ayub Khan already and especially since the execution of Ali Buttho they have retained this privilege. The aim of Kabul and Washington was to get rid of the Taliban sanctuaries in Pakistan. Pakistan and the USA were allies whose interests did not coincide.

Some thinkers in the USA also argued that Pakistan was the result of a disastrous marriage and that a divorce, that is to say splitting the country into several units, was to take place. They often felt worried because of the good relations between Islamabad and Beijing because China, once an ally of the North Americans against USSR, has since the collapse of USSR become a major world superpower and the most dangerous rival of the United States. Pakistan also clearly understood that India, as China's rival in Asia, was now

---

[48] Graham Usher, 'Liaisons dangereuses en Asie du Sud', in *Le Monde Diplomatique*, janvier 2009, p 10.
[49] Barack Obama, 'Reviewing American Leadership', in *Foreign Affairs*, New York, July–August, 2007, p 43.

close to become Washington favourite ally in South Asia and they decided to comply when asked by their powerful Godfather to do something about the "T". Most political thinkers in the United States have continuously seen Pakistan as a rogue state and only the struggle against Russia had made possible a deep alliance between the two countries but the time when the CIA and ISI exchanged information and worked together was, in the twenty-first century, a thing of the past.

As usual, the politicians, the Army and ISI did a half job to prevent dangerous confrontations and retain strategic positions. The Generals wanted the "T" as a terrorist group to be used in Kashmir and in the zone of the Durand line, the colonial border between Afghanistan and Pakistan. The politicians were afraid of ISI's creature (the "T"). So, 10,000 fighters were disbanded but, after some time, they reappeared in the charities of the movement and soon they were discretely reorganized and their recruiting agencies reopened in Punjab. The dismantled bases of the centre of Pakistan were re-installed in the North, close to the Taliban and their Pashtun allies. Some fighters and militants were jailed and released after a short spell. Pakistan could hardly do better: endless wars are sometimes a most convenient solution for a government. Had Pakistan got rid of these terrorist forces, India would have proved to the world and the UN that the Kashmir issue was settled in her favour once for all. Actually, the "T" was just less involved in Kashmir and South Asia and more involved in the Pashtun regions and especially on both sides of the Durand line where the Pashtun fought with the Taliban against the forces of Kabul and her Pashtun President. The contradictions were not only obvious on the Pakistani side, in Waziristan for instance the Taliban were backed by clans who did not want to fight against Pakistan.

It appeared that the normal alternation of the two main parties was re-established when Nawaz Sharif reconquered in 2013 the position of Prime Minister but he was accused of corruption when the Panama papers were published in 2017. His fortune abroad obviously came from stolen state funds in Pakistan. One year later, the elections showed that Pakistani people were tired of the two-party system. The rather poor South of Punjab had become more indifferent to the PML (which had become the PML(N) with "N" for Nawaz Sharif) and the North of Sindh less committed to PPP. When national politicians become less popular, peripheric aspirations become stronger and outsiders may have a chance to come to the front: the Balochi National Party was progressing, the Pashtun MMA (Majlis-e-Amal) banks of votes were tempted to follow Imran Khan, the candidate of the PTI (Pakistan Tehreek-e-Insaf), a man who was from their own region. The religious conservative Parties were on the decay and they hardly reached 10 %. Imran Khan, a former cricket star, won the polls.

This victory of an outsider can be explained by causes that show his strong points against the traditional politicians as well as the fact that he was only half an outsider.

In the twenty-first century the urban middle class favoured by liberal economics grew rapidly whereas the traditional politicians did not change very much. Imran Khan, as a younger man than his opponents and as the incarnation of a post-modern success story, skilfully appealed to this new class.

Although it did not win in Lahore and Karachi, the PTI nevertheless vied with the weakened great parties (MLP(N) and PPP) which used to dominate in these regions. The political landscape was shorn of the two political giants of the past: Benazir Buttho and Nawaz Sharif. Their personalities used to count more than their parties that were actually notorious for their corruption. In the absence of such charismatic leaders, the local roots (Sindh and Punjab) of their parties were likely to be erased. Each was weakened in the less prosperous parts of their strongholds, the North of Sindh for the PPP and the South of Punjab for the PML(N) and the PTI suddenly emerged as a mainstream Party, which had never been the case before.

The PPP and MLP(N) as well as their leaders struggled desperately with corruption cases.

In the Pashtun regions, PTI was extremely aggressive against the hold of the MLP(N) and the constituencies knew that Imran was a son of the soil. In Baluchistan, the local MLP(N) was imploding and Balochi Nationalist politicians were on a path of war against

Nawaz Sharif. They turned their backs to the MLP(N), expecting a better deal with Imran Khan.

The PTI leader and candidate got a discreet but efficient help from the Army whereas Nawaz Sharif had spoilt his relation with the Generals by accepting too confidently the US strategy of breaking the links between the politicians and the soldiers. He also accepted too easily a dialogue with India and, in the process, he probably yielded too much and too quickly to India, especially when he met the Indian Prime Minister, Modi, who is hated by the Pakistani army for his Hindu nationalist stances against Islam and Pakistan. The PTI did evoke the importance of a dialogue with India but it did so by using conventional terms for peace while also using very conventional hawkish terms about Kashmir and water treaties with India. Imran Khan was clearly conscious that to rule Pakistan he should never destroy the relation of confidence between him and the generals.

The conclusion is obviously that the so-called outsider looks very often very similar to the politicians of the past while adopting a very different style: he was different enough to look as a new man and appeal to the electors but not enough to break with the military and change Pakistan.

CONCLUSION

The desire to create an Islamic entity called Pakistan was strong and enduring but it was not in the hearts of most politicians as deep as in the hearts of Muslim intellectuals because for the ruling class it was the result of the fear of an independent Hindu India that brought them to the concept of an Islamic Republic. In their resolution the fear was probably superior to the faith. Third world countries often feel that their diversity might be a weakness and they look desperately for an ideology that would unite their various components and fill the gap between them and the people. Most often the ideological stance is unproductive if there is no development and no social progress. It is especially so if corruption and nepotism soil the national ideals. In Pakistan the version of Islam that prevailed was ideological in so far as an ideology is a system of thought that backs the interests of a group of people. When this group is an élite, the ideology is used to make the subalterns think like the rulers and accept their inferior status as deserved and necessary to the common good. Islam is obviously more than an ideology and its instrumentalization in Pakistan was a betrayal.

So, the intellectual tool used to rule and take decisions was twisted from the start. The answers given to national and international questions are actually answers which suit the will to prevail of the dominant classes and their various components (politicians, bureaucrats, business people, feudal forces...) more than answers which cope with the real problems raised at home or in the geographical, strategic and economic larger environment of the country.

For Pakistan these problems were (no one will deny it) incredibly difficult and complex. They involved economic questions, strategic issues, regional realities and global ones. Religions and cultures, ethnic and social differences related to different times: the time of the élite is linear but many classes and ethnic groups relate to a cyclic time; the bourgeois class relates to progress whereas the feudal lords are unwilling to throw away their traditional privileges; the working-class expects a better future coming from a break whereas the middle-classes accept most of the features and the global logic of the established economic system; the secularized élite trusts the present, the religious traditionalists trust the Golden Age of Islam and recreate a hybrid of past and present to oppose the religious progressive trends of Islam or the Kemalists... It is not only space which is dangerous for Pakistan, it is also time, but if we believe the national poet and philosopher Iqbal, time should not be a danger in so far as "God is time", which means that we should be open to change, creation and future.

There is no reason to think that Islam cannot cope with such a complexity but not an ideological and rigid version of Islam which is a simplification and a distortion. Some extremists might see the contradictions between Shi'ites and Sunnites as a very serious question, but the regional realities are perhaps more difficult to check. After all, the great founder, Jinnah, was born in a Shi'ite family. Iskander Mirza, whose role was so important to move from a civilian regime to a military one, was a Shi'ite, like Yayia Khan who was President of the Republic (1969–1971). The second Prime Minister of Pakistan and the third one belonged to this community. The Buttho Dynasty was Shi'ite too. Like the French Protestants of the sixteenth and seventeenth centuries, members of this important minority have often come to the conclusion that the best way to defend itself is to stress and serve faithfully the national identity and interests of Pakistan. Many Hindus (seven million and a rich community), Sikhs (300,000, mostly in Karachi), Christians and Zoroastrians of Pakistan think alike.

To be flexible and up to this incredibly difficult project that is called Pakistan, Islam has to use the tools of democracy and not only representative democracy which has been used in the Third world with almost no results, but also a participative version of this system of government. Panchayats or other institutions that were to bring about the voice of the rank and file have been very often manipulated or weakened by bureaucrats or private interests but they would require very little change to become more efficient: only a withdrawal of the administration in the election of the rulers and the gift of judicial rights to challenge the rich and the bureaucrats would be enough to help tremendously Panchayats to change the lives of the poor. Most often the Panchayats are seen as relays of the decisions taken by the central or regional powers at the top. The task is difficult but Pakistan, to become a more united nation instead of staying a still divided protonation, must overcome the cruel inequalities between rich and poor and eradicate the poverty and despair of so many commoners and subalterns. In such a process Islam will dig out traditions and values which will provide solutions. All religions and cultures can provide them so that the best that they possess cannot be wiped away from history. The state which respects and backs grass-root movements with schools, clinics, social and financial help and active sympathy instead of scorn, hostility or indifference, will redeem itself but if it betrays them, it will dig its own tomb. In such a process from the base to the top, diversity and complexity cease being handicaps to become a rich and buoyant creative force.

Education is of course a key-sector. The Central State and the four provincial governments provide education to the population, backed by private schools and a network of Madrasas. The 11 years of compulsory education still leave five million and a half children without any schooling, particularly girls (they are more than 60 % of the children who do not go to school). Primary schools welcome only 74 % of the children who should be welcome at that level. Only 44 % of them will reach the secondary level (middle schools and high schools). The higher levels, intermediate, undergraduate degrees, graduate degrees, are practically for a thin élite. Only 56 % of Pakistani people can read and write. Teachers are badly paid. Local Lords sometimes take over school premises for their cattle.[50] The network of schools clearly favours the East (with Punjab and Sindh) against the West.[51]

The health budget is only 2.5 of the BIP. The Centre has withdrawn from this sector in 2011 and the regions are fully responsible, but actually the situation is now even worse than before: 80 % of medical services are private (which often means very costly), the state hospitals are badly equipped, Mothers' death rates are high

---

[50] Tasnim Altaf Butt, op. cit., p 119.
[51] Ibid., p 131.

(2.6 /1000), death rates for very young children are around 6 %, many diseases are connected with a weak nutrition, the number of doctors for inhabitants is 0.8, rural regions are deprived of most medical cares.[52]

The latest example of the inadequacy of social services and even of the central State appeared in 2020 during the Covid19 epidemics. The experience of the SARS disease in 2003 could have helped hospitals and politicians to cope with Covid19 but in fact the services and government were found unprepared. Huge rallies protested against the confusion and bad management of the crisis in most big cities. By November statistics published on the internet by the Advisory Platform by the Ministry of Health were that the number of victims amounted to 333,970 serious cases and 6,890 deaths. More than four million people have been tested. Some evaluations propose that the official number of cases should be multiplied by ten and the number of the dead by three. Others say that not 10 % of the population is infected (official evaluation) but rather 25 %. Lockdowns organized in big cities could have been more efficient but it was very difficult to go against some social constraints like poverty, poor health and overpopulated houses and habits like family meetings and hugging of all the people present at funerals. Superstitions have also created problems: hostility against the people, who had contracted the disease, prejudices against vaccination (the rumour was that the components of vaccines include pork), accusation against doctors, patients hiding because of the supposed indignity attached to the disease and even the rather stupid rumour of a Jewish plot behind the world epidemics. It is necessary to point at the responsibilities of politicians and the weaknesses of social services available like the health service of course but also education which provides better hygienic habits and fewer superstitions that can sometimes ruin the efforts of dedicated doctors and nurses.

The law against blasphemy is still a key problem because it seems that it cannot be handled. It comes from a colonial law (1885) that Jinnah rejected. General Zia imposed this law to court the most conservative sectors of the Pakistani population. The "T" makes it

---

[52] Ibid., p 120.

the instrument of its terrorist policy. Some people use it to get rid of rivals. Most accused are subsequently innocent, but when the accused is declared not guilty, he is likely to be murdered (it was the case of two Christian brothers declared not guilty). Members of the minorities (3 to 5 %) are the accused in 40 % of the cases. Muslims are also victimized (60 % of the cases). The list of victims is long (Rao Iqbal, Youssaf Bei, Manzoor Masih, Asia Bibi, Junaid Hafa...) and it spoils the repute of Pakistan. Those who want to improve the law are threatened and sometimes murdered (Shahaz Bhali, Salman Taziz...). The project to pass a law against false accusations is rejected by the "T". Imran Khan seems to court the conservative vote and is not very likely to stand against this law which is continuously manipulated by unscrupulous people and forces.

The twenty-first century has brought a new urge in human ecology. Pakistan has been struck by heat waves which paralyzed the country and killed thousands of exhausted citizens. The Indus is no longer flowing to the sea. The people who lived on the banks are losing their reliant way of life, connected villages are more and more disconnected, farmers, fishermen, small traders and boatmen are losing their jobs. Textiles and mines pollute the land and the water, poison and kill people, they spread cancers, breathing diseases and bone deformations at birth. To cope with such realities regional cooperation is necessary and local initiatives also for democracy (representative and participative), social justice (let us never forget that the very rich pollute much more than the poor), a fair judicial system open to the poor, the rights of women and minorities and regional peace.

Fortunately, Pakistanis are courageous people with a long experience of struggle against dictatorial regimes and authoritarian forms of pseudo-democracy. The press is bold, the resources of internet are frequently used, the critical sense is sharp, and journalists work seriously in spite of constant threats (including murders). Newspaper are bold and diverse: *News* the first English speaking paper, *Dawn / Herald,* created by Jinnah in 1941, *The Nation, Nawa-e-waqt,* an old Urdu newspaper, *Daily Jang,* perhaps the most popular of all... TV channels (among them PTV), private networks (*Geo,*

Ary) and radios are flourishing in spite of the tense political environment of the country. Sufi songs and ghazals are still very important in daily life and young singers are following the path opened by Noor Jahan (1926–2000). Lollywood (from Lahore) is still a modest cinema industry and some people raise objections about the moral influence of this art, but others dream of successes comparable to the most prestigious achievements of Bollywood. The situation from this point of view is very different from what it was under Zia and the change is due to the courage of intellectuals and unionists although it is only fair to remember that Musharraf had a responsibility in the liberation of media. Harshly criticized by those to whom he had given a voice, he became one of the victims of this change but no improvement of people's freedom must be restrained once it is granted.

In the Islamic Golden Age, ideas were flourishing, social and democratic trends were growing in Bagdad. The Muslim invented the income tax and the terms left and right to describe the political groups debating on social and political issues. New institutions were springing in Cairo and Cordoba (schools, universities, hospitals…). The kings were responsible for "grass and water" and very rarely did they try to separate workers from their tools and means of production.

Some people might be tempted to describe Pakistan as a hopeless State but the vitality and the courage of many citizens and the rich and diverse cultural base of this country speak against such an undeserved statement.

BIBLIOGRAPHY

Abbasi, Muhammad Y., *The Genesis of Muslim Fundamentalism in British India*, Eastern Book Corporation, New Delhi, 1987

Abed al-Jabi, Mohamed, *Introduction à la critique de la pensée arabe*, Découverte, Paris, 1994

Armstrong, Karen, *Islam: A Short History*, Phoenix, London, 2000

Aziz, Khursheed K., *The Making of Pakistan: A Study in Nationalism*, Chattos & Windus, London, 1967

Banerjee, Anil C., *Two Nations: The Philosophy of Muslim Nationalism*, Concept Publishing Company, New Delhi, 1981

Belmekki, Belkacem, "Shah Walyi Allah Delhavi's Attempts at Religious Revivalism in South Asia", in *Anthropos: International Review of Anthropology and Linguistics*, N° 109/2, Anthropos Institut, Germany, 2014 (pp. 621–625)

Bergson, Henri, *Les deux sources de la morale et de la religion*, PUF, Paris, 1958

Bider, Abdennour, *L'Islam face à la mort de Dieu*, François Bourin, Paris, 2010

Butt, Altaf Tasmin, *Pakistan*, de Boek, Louvain-la-Neuve, 2014

Cohen, S. P., *The Idea of Pakistan*, Brookings, Wash. D.C., 2004

Dessart, Laurent, *Les pashtouns*, L'Harmattan, Paris, 2001

Gandhi, Rajmohan, *Understanding the Muslim Mind*, Penguin Books India, New Delhi, 1987

Haqqani, Husein, *Pakistan Between Mosque and the Military*, Carnegie, Wash. D.C., 2005

Hardy, Peter, *The Muslims of British India*, COP, Cambridge, 1972

Hocquert, Denis, *Zalfar Ali, le premier des Buttho*, L'Harmattan, Paris, 2009

Jaffrelot, Christophe, *Le Carrefour des tensions régionales*, Complexe, Bruxelles, 2002

Jaffrelot, Christophe, *Le Pakistan*, Fayard, Paris, 2000

Jalal, Ayesha, *The Sole Spokesman*, CUP, Cambridge, 1994

Khan, Yasmin, *The Great Partition*, Yale University Press, New Haven, 2008

Malik, Hafeez, *Sir Sayyid Ahmad Khan and Muslim Modernization in India and Pakistan*, Columbia University Press, New York, 1980

Malik, Iftikar, *Culture and Customs of Pakistan*, Greenwood, Westport, 2006

Malik, Iftikar, *History of Pakistan*, Greenwood Press, Wesport, 2008

Masselos, Jim, *Indian Nationalism: An History*, Sterling Publishers Private Limited, New Delhi, 1996

Muhammad, Shan, *Writings and Speeches of Sir Syed Ahmad Khan*, Nachiketa Publications Limited, Bombay, 1972

Naumann, Michel, *MN Roy*, L'Harmattan, Paris, 2006

Roy, Olivier et Abou Zahab, Maiam, *Réseaux islamiques: la connexion afghano-pakistanaise*, CERI, Paris, 2002

Sahu, B. P., *Iron and Social Change in Early India*, OUP, New Delhi, 2006

Sharif, Mian M., *A History of Muslim Philosophy: With Short Accounts of Other Disciplines and the Modern Renaissance in Muslim Lands* (Vol II), Otto Harrassowitz, Wiesbaden, Germany, 1966

Singh, Jawant, *Jinnah*, OUP, Oxford, 2009

Spear, Percival, *A History of India: From the Sixteenth Century to the Twentieth Century*, Penguin Books, Middlesex, 1990

Talbot, Ian, *Pakistan, a Modern History*, St Martin's Press, New York, 1998

Wasti, Syed Razi, 'British Policy towards the Indian Muslims Immediately after 1857', S. R. Wasti (ed.), Renaissance Publishing House, Delhi, 1993 (1–24)

Wolpert, Stanley, *Jinnah of Pakistan*, OUP, New York, 1984

Zins, Max-Jean, *Pakistan, la quête de l'identité*, Documentation française, Paris, 2002

Ziring, Lawrence, *Pakistan in the Twentieth Century*, OUP, Karachi, 1997

APPENDIXES

Jinnah's 14 points established in 1929 about the coming independence of India:

1. The form of the future constitution should be federal with the residuary powers rested in the provinces.
2. A uniform measure of autonomy shall be granted to all provinces.
3. All legislative in the country and other elected bodies shall be constituted on the definite principles of adequate and effective representation of minorities in every province without reducing the majority in any province to a minority or even equality.
4. In the central legislative, Muslims representative shall be not less than one-third.
5. Representative of communal groups shall continue to be by means of separate electorates as at present provided it shall be open to any community, at any time to abandon its separate electorate in favour of joint electorate.
6. Any territorial re-distribution that might at any time be necessary shall not in any way, affect the Muslim majority in Punjab, Bengal and N.W.F.P.
7. Full religious Liberty, liberty of belief, worship and observance, association and education shall be guaranteed to all the communication.
8. No bill or resolution shall be passed in any legislative or any other elected body if three-fourths of the members of any community in that particular body oppose such a bill.
9. Sindh should be separated from Bombay Presidency.
10. Reforms should be introduced in the North-West Frontier Province and Baluchistan on the same footing as in other provinces.
11. Muslims should be given adequate share along with other Indians in the services of State.

12. The constitution should embody adequate safeguard for the protection of Muslim culture, language, religion and civilization.
13. No cabinet, either central or provincial be formed. Without being a proportion of at least one-third Muslim Ministers.
14. No change shall be made in the constitution of state except with the concurrence of State constituting the Indian Federation.

Jinnah and the Constitution of Pakistan:

Mr. President, Ladies and Gentlemen!
I cordially thank you, with the utmost sincerity, for the honour you have conferred upon me — the greatest honour that is possible for this Sovereign Assembly to confer — by electing me as your first President. I also thank those leaders who have spoken in appreciation of my services and [thank them for] their personal references to me. I sincerely hope that with your support and your co-operation we shall make this Constituent Assembly an example to the world. The Constituent Assembly has got two main functions to perform. The first is the very onerous and responsible task of framing the future constitution of Pakistan and the second of functioning as a full and complete sovereign body as the Federal Legislature of Pakistan. We have to do the best we can in adopting a provisional constitution for the Federal Legislature of Pakistan. You know really that not only we ourselves are wondering but, I think, the whole world is wondering at this unprecedented cyclonic revolution which has brought about the plan of creating and establishing two independent Sovereign Dominions in this sub-continent. As it is, it has been unprecedented; there is no parallel in the history of the world. This mighty sub-continent with all kinds of inhabitants has been brought under a plan which is titanic, unknown, unparalleled. And what is very important with regard to it is that we have achieved it peacefully and by means of an evolution of the greatest possible character.

Dealing with our first function in this Assembly, I cannot make any well-considered pronouncement at this moment, but I shall say a few things as they occur to me. The first and the foremost thing that I would like to emphasize is this: remember that you are now a Sovereign Legislative body and you have got all the powers. It therefore places on you the gravest responsibility as to how you should take your decisions. The first observation that I would like to make is this: You will no doubt agree with me that the first duty of a government is to maintain law and order, so that the life, property and religious beliefs of its subjects are fully protected by the State.

The second thing that occurs to me is this: One of the biggest curses from which India is suffering — I do not say that other countries are free from it, but I think our condition is much worse — is bribery and corruption. That really is a poison. We must put that down with an iron hand, and I hope that you will take adequate measures as soon as it is possible for this Assembly to do so.

Black-marketing is another curse. Well, I know that black-marketeers are frequently caught and punished. Judicial sentences are passed, or sometimes fines only are imposed. Now you have to tackle this monster, which today is a colossal crime against society, in our distressed conditions, when we constantly face shortage of food and other essential commodities of life. A citizen who does black-marketing commits, I think, a greater crime than the biggest and most grievous of crimes. These black-marketeers are really knowing, intelligent, and ordinarily responsible people, and when they indulge in black-marketing, I think they ought to be very severely punished, because they undermine the entire system of control and regulation of foodstuffs and essential commodities, and cause wholesale starvation and want and even death.

The next thing that strikes me is this: Here again it is a legacy which has been passed on to us. Along with many other things, good and bad, has arrived this great evil — the evil of nepotism and jobbery. I want to make it quite clear that I shall never tolerate any kind of jobbery [=corrupt employment practices], nepotism, or any influence directly or indirectly brought to bear upon me. Whenever I will find that such a practice is in vogue or is continuing anywhere, low or high, I shall certainly not countenance it.

I know there are people who do not quite agree with the division of India and the partition of the Punjab and Bengal. Much has been said against it, but now that it has been accepted, it is the duty of every one of us to loyally abide by it and honourably act according to the agreement which is now final and binding on all. But you must remember, as I have said, that this mighty revolution that has taken place is unprecedented. One can quite understand the feeling that exists between the two communities wherever one community is in majority and the other is in minority. But the question is, whether it was possible or practicable to act otherwise than what has been done. A division had to take place. On both sides, in Hindustan and Pakistan, there are sections of people who may not agree with it, who may not like it; but in my judgement there was no other solution, and I am sure future history will record its verdict in favour of it. And what is more, it will be proved by actual experience as we go on that that was the only solution of India's constitutional problem. Any idea of a united India could never have worked, and in my judgement, it would have led us to terrific disaster. Maybe that view is correct; maybe it is not; that remains to be seen. All the same, in this division it was impossible to avoid the question of minorities being in one Dominion or the other. Now that was unavoidable. There is no other solution. Now what shall we do? Now, if we want to make this great State of Pakistan happy and prosperous, we should wholly and solely concentrate on the well-being of the people, and especially of the masses and the poor. If you will work in co-operation, forgetting the past, burying the hatchet, you are bound to succeed. If you change your past and work together in a spirit that every one of you, no matter to what community he belongs, no matter what relations he had with you in the past, no matter what is his colour, caste, or creed, is first, second, and last a citizen of this State with equal rights, privileges, and obligations, there will be no end to the progress you will make.

I cannot emphasize it too much. We should begin to work in that spirit, and in course of time all these angularities of the majority and minority communities, the Hindu community and the Muslim community — because even as regards Muslims you have Pathans, Punjabis, Shias, Sunnis and so on, and among the Hindus you have Brahmins, Vashnavas, Khatris, also Bengalees, Madrasis and so on — will vanish. Indeed, if you ask me, this has been the biggest hindrance in the way of India to attain the freedom and independence, and but for this we would have been free people long ago. No power can hold another nation, and specially a nation of 400 million souls, in subjection; nobody could have conquered you, and even if it had happened, nobody could have continued its hold on you for any length of time, but for this. Therefore, we must learn a lesson from this. You are free; you are free to go to your temples; you are free to go to your mosques or to any other place or worship in this State of Pakistan. You may belong to any religion or caste or creed — that has nothing to do with the business of the State. As you know, history shows that in England conditions, some time ago, were much worse than those prevailing in India today. The Roman Catholics and the Protestants persecuted each other. Even now there are some States in existence where there are discriminations made and bars imposed against a particular class. Thank God, we are not starting in those days. We are starting in the days where there is no discrimination, no distinction between one community and another, no discrimination between one caste or creed and another. We are starting with this fundamental principle: that we are all citizens, and equal citizens, of one State. The people of England in [the] course of time had to face the realities of the situation, and had to discharge the responsibilities and burdens placed upon them by the government of their country; and they went through that fire step by step. Today, you might say with justice that Roman Catholics and Protestants do not exist; what exists now is that every man is a citizen, an equal citizen of Great Britain, and they are all members of the Nation.

Now I think we should keep that in front of us as our ideal, and you will find that in course of time Hindus would cease to be Hindus, and Muslims would cease to be Muslims, not in the religious sense, because that is the personal faith of each individual, but in the political sense as citizens of the State.

Well, gentlemen, I do not wish to take up any more of your time; and thank you again for the honour you have done to me. I shall always be guided by the principles of justice and fair play without any, as is put in the political language, prejudice or ill-will; in other words, partiality or favouritism. My guiding principle will be justice and complete impartiality, and I am sure that with your support and co-operation, I can look forward to Pakistan becoming one of the greatest Nations of the world.

I have received a message from the United States of America addressed to me. It reads: I have the honour to communicate to you, in Your Excellency's capacity as President of the Constituent Assembly of Pakistan, the following message which I have just received from the Secretary of State of the United States:

On the occasion of the first meeting of the Constituent Assembly for Pakistan, I extend to you and to the members of the Assembly, the best wishes of the Government and the people of the United States for the successful conclusion of the great work you are about to undertake.

Cardinal Coutts on Minorities in Pakistan (11/8/2019):

> A Pakistani Bishop committed suicide (although it's not allowed by the Church) in the past to protest against the betrayal of Jinnah's dream of Pakistan. A Christian Minister recently created a minority day to revive this dream. He was murdered some time later. Bishop Coutts is following the track of these Pakistanis who, like most citizens of this country want to be faithful to the Father of the Nation.

The founder of Pakistan Mohammad Ali Jinnah in his historic speech of August 11, 1947, assured us that people of faith other than Islam would be citizens of Pakistan, with equal rights and duties. Consequently, we should be treated as equal citizens of Pakistan for all the 365 days of the year, without the need to have a Day for Religious Minorities in Pakistan."

This is what Cardinal Joseph Coutts, Archbishop of Karachi told Fides News Agency. Cardinal Coutts, renowned for his commitment to promoting peace and harmony in Pakistan, on the occasion of Minorities Day, celebrated on August 11 throughout the country, told Fides: "We people are Pakistanis, we are not migrants from any other country, we were born and raised in Pakistan and have lived here for centuries before Pakistan's independence. We should not be treated as second-class citizens."

We have contributed to the development of the country since the first day of its independence. And we still do it today: the Pakistani Catholic Bishops' Conference has responded to Prime Minister Imran Khan's appeal for the construction of water basins and dams in Pakistan and we have collected donations from all our Pakistani Christians.

"We should be treated as citizens equal to others and not as religious minorities in Pakistan. I appreciate Prime Minister Imran Khan for strongly opposing forced conversions in his speech of July 30, 2019, while celebrating Minorities Day. It seems that this government is aware of the challenges of the people of religious minorities in Pakistan. It is a positive sign; we ask to guarantee the protection of religious minorities and the places of worship of religious minorities.

Map of the Indian Subcontinent in 1947

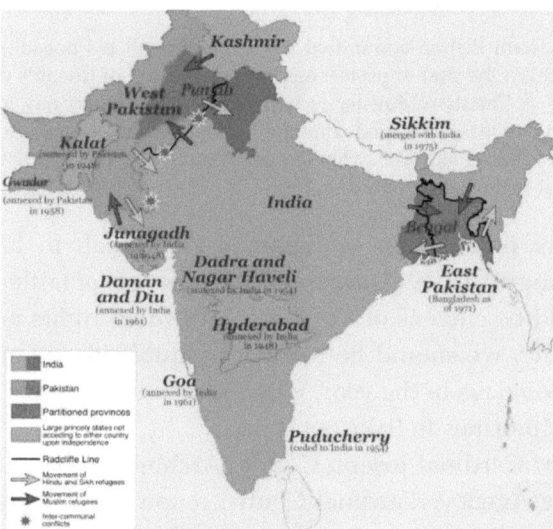

Map of the partition of India (1947). Note: Small princely states not acceding to either country upon independence are shown as integral parts of India and Pakistan. (c) Wikimedia Commons, CC BY-SA 4.0, https://commons.wikimedia.org/wiki/File:Partition_of_India_1947_en.svg#file

Languages and regions of Pakistan

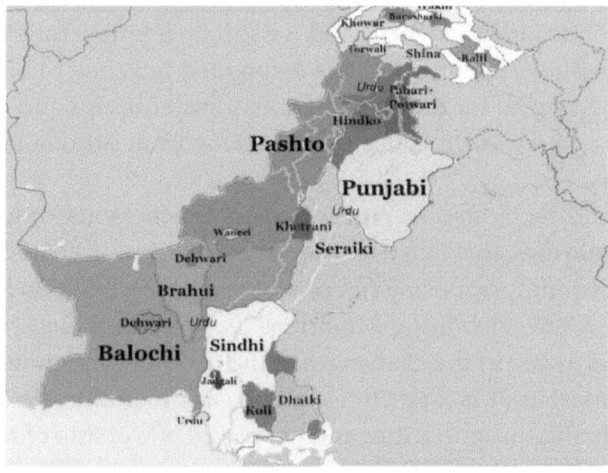

Languages of Pakistan. (c) Ameerhamzaabbasi, via Wikimedia Commons, CC BY-SA 3.0, https://creativecommons.org/licenses/by-sa/3.0

***ibidem**.eu*